MONEY MANAGEMENT *for* MINISTERS

by

Manfred Holck Jr.

Augsburg Publishing House · Minneapolis, Minnesota

MONEY MANAGEMENT FOR MINISTERS

Copyright © 1966 Augsburg Publishing House

Library of Congress Catalog Card No. 66-22559

MANUFACTURED IN THE UNITED STATES OF AMERICA

To my wife
LOIS

*who shares with me
the responsibilities
of managing a
minister's money.*

CONTENTS

The Minister and His Money

Ministers spend their money the same as most people do. They support their families, provide for food and clothing, take out insurance, operate an automobile (maybe two), enjoy recreation and entertainment, and contribute to their church. However, there are some things ministers do not spend their money on. Many of them are not bothered with house payments or with utilities, escrow accounts and home improvements, because their churches provide a house and take care of these items for them.

Yet ministers do have financial responsibilities: They must plan their own insurance programs, keep their own financial records, have their own bank accounts, borrow money for a new car, and make their own wills. Since most businessmen deal with some or all of these matters quite frequently, many of them are experienced in handling them. Clergymen, on the other hand, are frequently uninformed, inexperienced, and untrained in many of the financial affairs of the business world simply because their involvement is neither as frequent nor as extensive. Nevertheless, a minister must deal with many of these matters in his personal finances, albeit infrequently, whether he likes it or not.

Of course, each minister's life is different and unique. We all have our own peculiar likes and dislikes. Incomes and obligations vary, tastes and attitudes are not the same, responsibilities and ambitions differ. How ministers use their money is very much dependent on such things as salary, community, congregational expectations, family ambitions, age.

1

Although the image of a minister may be somewhat stereotyped, few persons expect all preachers to be identical either in their preaching or their spending. Some preach superbly, others are only average. Some save wisely, others spend foolishly. But all of them are called to preach, and every one of them uses his money for one purpose or another.

Stories are told of ministers "taken for a ride" by some smooth, fast-talking salesman and being duped out of their life's savings for worthless gold mine investments, retirement utopias, "preferred" stocks, and bold, get-rich-quick schemes. Professional men in other occupations have probably been equally unfortunate. But if dependable statistics could be compiled on the number of such ruinations, one might be surprised at the preponderance of naive and consequently "skinned-alive" preachers over other professional men.

The typical young unmarried minister-to-be, for instance, will care less about finances—or at least proper budgeting and careful spending of the few resources he has—than he will about intellectual growth and the attainment of his ambitions for ordination. Perhaps that is the way it should be. But an in-seminary marriage will often wake up a seminarian to newly created financial obligations. And the ordained minister and his family, as intensely committed to the Gospel ministry as they may be, all too frequently know very little about getting along in the world of business and finance.

Spending money intelligently in a world where business is business from Monday to Saturday, no matter how eloquently or passionately the pulpit rings with pleas to the contrary, is not easy. And in a world like this, the minister, be he fresh from seminary or four-score-years wise, must be able to speak and act intelligently about his money. Otherwise, the often inadequate salary he earns will not stretch to meet his needs.

Dedicated churchmen will often offer professional advice to their pastors if they ask for it, and without a fee, too. But they seldom take the time to sit down in the living room of their pastor's home to discuss frankly with him the matter of budgeting, discounts, wills, insurance, investments, and all such financial and legal matters. The businessman takes these things for granted. He assumes everyone knows about checking accounts, installment sales, stocks, and bonds, because he deals with them every day. Too often too late the minister comes to the trusted businessman to ask for help.

Of course, there are thousands upon thousands of clergymen who are able to "make do" with their salaries, no matter how much or how little they earn. But many of these might have done better, might have been pushed less often toward financial chaos and have saved more of their hard-earned cash, had they been informed or known where to go for counsel.

Obviously, in an outline of helps such as this book presents, specific financial information for particular instances may be lacking, but it is hoped that some basic general information can be given. Such information can be very useful to the minister who is eager to spend wisely the money he has, as well as to provide for the other financial concerns all men face in our society.

It is hoped that in the pages that follow considerable help will be given to those clergymen who are eager to make the most of their money but whose business sense is no match for the rest of the world. Let it be said emphatically, though, that final decisions on important legal and financial matters ought to be made only upon the advice of experts in such matters, such as lawyers, bankers, investment counselors. The suggestions listed in these pages are intended only for guidance and not as the last word on how a minister ought to spend his money. Each man must ultimately make that decision for himself. But an intelligent decision can be made only on the basis of an informed evaluation of all the alternatives involved.

After all, ministers cannot live successfully aloof from money matters. Our society is no longer so ordered that a man's needs—any man's needs—are simply and easily met. The very fact that clergymen earn a salary and thus have money to spend, no matter how much or how little, puts them right alongside the millions of other people who also have money to spend and who must cope with many of the same kinds of money problems. Ministers cannot run away from their responsibilities to manage that money wisely as stewards of that which God has given to them.

Ministers, therefore, must manage their money one way or another. Some will do the job rather haphazardly, with predictable disaster. Others will do it well and reap the benefits which come from wise and prudent money management—workable family budgets, sensible accumulations of furnishings, realistic and fruitful savings and investment plans, well-planned insurance programs, intelligent retirement goals. But only with diligence, perseverance, self-discipline, and a few practical guidelines to follow can money management be fruitful and satisfying, not to say beneficial, for any family. It is hoped that these pages will provide guidelines for ministers and their families for managing their money.

The author is indebted to many people for their encouragement and advice in this effort, especially to Kenneth E. Broin, assistant vice-president, First National Bank of Minneapolis, who offered many helpful suggestions about budgeting, banking and investments; to Roland C. Matthies, J.D., vice-president and treasurer, Wittenberg University, Springfield, Ohio, for his suggestions on charitable gift annuities, wills, and other legal matters; to Donald H. Barkley, agent for Lutheran Mutual Life Insurance Company and candidate for Certified Life Underwriter designation, who offered valuable advice on insurance; to my father, Manfred Holck Sr., senior partner, Barr, Howard, Boswell and Holck, Certified Public Accountants, Austin, Texas, who reviewed the entire manuscript with special emphasis on matters related to savings and loan associations, budgeting, and taxes; and to my wife, who has diligently proofread the typescript and regularly added her words of encouragement. Indeed, this book has come about because she insisted that our family develop a sensible money management scheme. The following pages outline the principles of that plan.

MANFRED HOLCK JR.

Chapter 1

Family Budgeting

A quick glance at the financial records of some ministers' families will reveal almost negligible budgeting plans. Not only ministers' families, but most families, are quite lax in planning an intelligent, systematic use of their money. Too often their spending is limited only by income that happens to be available at the moment. That kind of buying is frequently done on the basis of immediate desire or spontaneous appeal rather than on real need and common sense. In too many families there is seldom any intentional planning for financing and installment buying, except to acknowledge that one's income is already strained and thus the lower the monthly payment the better, no matter how many months or years or extra costs are involved.

Budgeting helps to set reasonable limits on spending through intensive and careful financial planning, including current expenses, future savings, investments, and appliance purchases. Set up properly, a family budget will, among other things, assist parents in planning for their children's education, in providing for their own retirement, and in giving them a true picture of where the money goes (as well as how fast it goes). A budget can actually help a family save money and at the same time stretch its dollars further no matter how meager the available resources. Of course, any volunteer program of budget preparation and subsequent spending such as this must be done conscientiously and honestly if it is to be reasonably successful. There is not much purpose in budgeting if a family refuses to abide by the obvious implications which the program spells out for their spending.

5

Any budget, whether for a church or a business or a family, is often guesswork and after all only an estimate, but it ought to be an intelligent "guesstimate," a projected direction in which to go. Budgets are based on experience, on the past records of income and expenses, as well as on future ambitions and goals. They should be flexible, subject to change as circumstances change, for they are simply guides, helps, programs intended to give direction and purpose for the intelligent spending of funds.

Thus, the first inclusive budget a family ever prepares is likely to be considerably different from subsequent budgets it may develop. When families begin the process of keeping accurate, dependable financial records, they soon discover how their first guesswork budget involved some misconceptions about where they thought all that money went each month! But at least this is the beginning. After several months of keeping accurate records of all the pennies and nickles, and dollar bills, too, a family may finally get its head above water, and all the time and effort spent for budgeting begins to make sense. For out of it all comes a rather dependable record of what that family is doing with its income. And while even these results may present a rather dismal picture of a seemingly hopeless situation, where outgo is still always more than income, at least the family knows why and ought to be able to take some intelligent steps to correct the situation.

Of course, changing our habits of spending and being satisfied with what we have rather than always wanting more—even if the payments are only $10 a month!—is never easy. Family budgeting, wherever it is tried, can give the direction and the reason and the intentions to make such changes. But no matter how good the budget, only the determination of the family involved can carry it out successfully.

Actually a family ought to consider two budgets—one, a detailed listing of the average expenses expected each month for the year, and the other, a listing of cash needs for each month of the year.

A family ought to know, for example, how much it spends for groceries and rent and insurance and entertainment, on the average, each month. But because not all family expenditures are paid out regularly each month, if there is no budget or spending plan, most families simply are unable to anticipate the several irregular payments which are suddenly due the next month or the month after that. Cash needs do differ from month to month. A substantial balance of cash in the checking account at the end of one month may or may not be encouraging. The annual car insurance payment may very well be due that next month, not to mention a quarterly income tax payment or the second semiannual installment on a son's college tuition.

Many family expenditures are of this kind, due annually or semiannually or quarterly. Obviously it takes careful planning to build up a sufficient cash reserve so that funds will be readily available when that kind of payment is due. A family must plan not only its average monthly spending goals, but it must also give serious thought to its monthly cash needs.

Preparing the Family Budget

The preparation of an average monthly budget will start with a listing of all the anticipated available sources of income for the entire calendar year. Most important, of course, will be the family's regular income, which is essentially the annual salary earned plus various allowances provided. While the various deductions regularly made by the salary-paying organization are a part of the family's expenses, nevertheless, for purposes of budgeting it is sufficient to begin with net take-home pay.

Then, other anticipated income can be listed: honorariums, fees, royalties, wife's part-time income, earnings from other employment, cash gifts. As complete and as accurate a listing as possible is important if a family expects to know how much will be available for its spending. And if all reasonably anticipated income is listed, not just salary earned, then a realistic spending budget for the family can be prepared.

The total of all these items, divided by twelve of course, will furnish the monthly spending limits for the family. The family's budget expenses will then be limited by this amount, for it is obviously foolish to budget more than one's anticipated income.

Next, a listing of all the items for which the family normally spends its money should be made. This should include the regular fixed items first, those regular expenses for which the family is committed and which cannot be easily changed; irregular fixed expenses, those fixed expenses which do not occur on a regular monthly basis; and finally, the flexible expenses, those items for which the family's tastes, desires, ambitions, and resources determine the amounts spent.

A partial listing of such items[1] would include:

> *Regular income:* salary, allowances, other
> *Irregular income:* fees, honorariums, royalties, gifts, other
> *Regular expenses:*
>   Contributions—church, charities
>   Savings—emergency fund, future fund, dream fund
>   Unexpected expense reserve fund
>   Housing payments—rent or mortgage, home owner's insurance policy premiums, taxes
>   Utilities—heat, electricity, telephone, water
>   Installment loan payments—furniture, appliances, car, other
>   Food (could also be considered a flexible expense)—at home, away from home, party food and beverages
>   Other personal items
> *Irregular expenses:*
>   Insurance—life, car, health, other
>   Taxes—federal income, state and city income, Social Security self-employment, other
>   Dues and subscriptions
>   Tuitions and fees
>   Vacations
>   Medicines, doctors' and dentists' fees

---

[1]Adapted from *Personal Money Management,* First National Bank of Minneapolis.

Home maintenance and improvement
Other repairs
Flexible expenses:
House operations—supplies, yard help, maintenance
Clothing—purchases, cleaning and repairs
Transportation—out-of-pocket car expenses, school bus fare, other transportation
Recreation—hobbies, dates, sports, pets, boats, books, music, theater, records
Personal care—barber shop and beauty parlor expenses, cosmetics, personal grooming items
Gifts
Education—school supplies, special courses, educational material
Miscellaneous—postage, stationery, small unclassified items

Then, using a form similar to that illustrated below for a proposed spending plan work sheet, list the total amounts spent during the past year for each item in the first column. This information may not be readily available if this is a first attempt at budget-making and if record-keeping has been neglected. But there must be a starting place. When actual expenditure records are unavailable, an estimate should be made. In subsequent months, as records are kept, a budget based on such estimates can be adjusted to the more correct amounts.

Nevertheless, when the best available sources of information have been used to determine probable expenditures for each item for the past year, total the first column. This amount should be close to what last year's expenditures, as well as income, actually were.

PROPOSED SPENDING PLAN WORK SHEET

Item	Total spent last year	Estimated expenses next year	Adjustments	Adjusted total	Average monthly spending expected

Then, in preparing your new budget, list those regular and irregular expenses that are precisely fixed and which will not change, or at
least cannot be easily changed. Adapt the sample listing to your own
circumstances since obviously there will be differences of opinion on
which items should be included and into which category they should
be placed. Even though a minister's contributions to his church and
charities may very well be listed in the category of regular expenses,
such contributions are certainly not a contractual obligation, legally,
and can be changed either upwards or downwards according to the
changes in a family's circumstances. And while the amount of savings
can be altered at any time, regular fixed payments to a savings plan
are vitally important to a family. In another chapter a realistic savings plan is suggested.

Next list the flexible expenditures, those items on which adjustments can more easily be made and for which a family can adapt its
habits and needs. For instance, groceries may be a fixed amount, as
shown in the previous listing. We all have to eat and we do so quite
regularly! But careful planning and more selective shopping, watch-
ing of ads, being particular about prices, and doing without some
items can have a considerable effect on the price of feeding a family.
Grocery costs may therefore be considered variable also. Other adjust-
able expenses would include entertainment, gifts, car expenses, and
so forth.

Flexible expenses added for the first time this year are to be encouraged if the family's resources permit. These might include new hobbies, a vacation trip, new appliances or furniture, increased contributions to the church, or a host of other things the family wants to
do and have if it can. Of course, for purposes of budget estimates
such amounts must represent reasonable desires and come within
the total anticipated income resources.

Then add it all up and compare these amounts with your total
anticipated income for the year; determine the difference, above or
below; then begin the painful (if a decrease is necessary) or pleasant
(if estimated income exceeds these cost estimates) process of adjust-

ing estimated expenditures to income. Extend these adjusted amounts to the next column; add it up—the total ought to equal income now; and then divide each item by twelve to arrive at the average monthly expenditures permissible for each item listed in this last column.

Now you should have a reasonable monthly estimate of what you will spend during the coming year, provided, of course, that your estimates are realistic and that your records of past experience are reasonably accurate. For the first several months of the new year significant adjustments may be necessary in this budget until a reliable pattern of spending is more accurately available. Nevertheless, this can be a helpful guide to those who are interested in making the most of their money.

As has been stated, if all of your expenditures were evenly divided from one month to the next month and every month's payments were exactly the same as your average monthly budget, family record keeping would be considerably simplified. But of course no one's expenses fall into that kind of regular pattern. Consequently, budgeting family expenses sometimes involves much more than estimating an average monthly spending pattern. Irregular fixed expenses, such as life insurance premiums and college tuition, must be anticipated, with sufficient cash available to pay them when they are due.

For the family that adheres closely to its planned spending program on an average expense budget, there may not be the temptation to spend for extras whenever a larger than usual cash balance appears in some months. Necessary cash funds will accumulate and be available when needed. But for others there is that temptation.

You may be interested in analyzing your cash needs more thoroughly. If so, a cash flow or cash outgo schedule can be quickly calculated. Such a schedule, actually a second budget, when completed will show you at a glance the approximate amount of cash you will need each month to meet your obligations as they are budgeted and as they come due.

In other words, your family's average monthly expense budget will indicate the average amount of cash you will need each month, but you will not necessarily spend that amount each month. Your annual insurance payment comes due only in one month. Your vocation expenses are paid seasonally not monthly. Proper budgeting of course will make provision for this, and cash will be available for these payments when they become due. But the cash flow chart will tell you how much actual cash you need each month. It will divide your annual budget into monthly cash needs rather than equal monthly expenses, so that the total cash you will need each month will be shown clearly. If you prefer this kind of planning, in addition to your average monthly family spending plan budget, you may want to develop some kind of work sheet similar to that illustrated below.

SPENDING PLAN CASH FLOW WORK SHEET

Item	Spending plan budget	Cash payments due in the month of—											
		J	F	M	A	M	J	J	A	S	O	N	D
Total cash needed each month													

Typical Living Costs for an Average Family

No one can predict exactly what any one family is likely to spend each month. Family spending is dependent on too many variable factors to be that predictable. There are wide differences in income, family size, tastes, ambitions, health, family responsibilities outside the immediate family, educational aims, and so forth. Over a period of time, however, each family ought to be able to predict rather well what its own spending habits will be. Budgeting helps to make such predictions.

For comparison the following information is presented simply as a guide to what "typical" families may spend each month. Your experience may be considerably different, so don't consider your spending unreasonable just because it fails to compare favorably with statistics. After all, your family's needs, desires, ambitions, and circumstances are different from those of your neighbor. Your budget is an individual thing with your family, and you simply cannot successfully fit your program into the straightjacket of someone else's ready-made budget. If you are conscientiously doing your best with family budgeting, and if your family is cooperating with you in this, then your plan is likely to be just as good, if not better, than any sample budget may be. However, if you are interested in guidelines for budget comparison, perhaps the following will be helpful.

One report of national averages suggests:

Household operation	12.2%
Clothing, accessories, jewelry	9.0%
Taxes	12.0%
Recreation	5.3%
Medical and dental	5.0%
Personal care and service	5.7%
Food and tobacco	23.0%
Transportation	9.1%
Housing	10.3%
Religion and welfare	2.0%
Savings	6.4%

Another report suggests that a family with a gross income of $400 a month and four dependents will spend on the average the following:

Federal Tax and Social Security	11.6%
Food	24.2%
Shelter	20.0%
House Operation	9.0%
Clothing	9.7%
Transportation	8.2%
Advancement	10.9%
Savings	6.4%

The United States Department of Agriculture Home and Garden Bulletin 98, *A Guide to Budgeting for the Young Couple,* estimates family spending as follows, for incomes above and below $5,000:

	Lower income Percent	Higher income Percent
Total money income	100	100
Total for current living	83	80
Food and beverages	19	18
Shelter (rent or mortgage payments and upkeep, insurance, and taxes)	13	12
Fuel and utilities	4	4
Household operations	5	5
Furnishings and equipment	5	4
Clothing	8	7
Transportation	15	16
Medical care	5	5
Recreation and education	5	5
Personal and miscellaneous	4	4
Gifts and contributions	3	3
Personal insurance	4	4
Income taxes	10	12
Savings	0	1

A comparison of these guides to spending points out the obvious differences between them and thus the inadequacy of their rigid use for your family's budget preparation. Your spending habits must be tailored to your own needs and ambitions. Good management of your money must be planned to fit the needs and wants of your family.

Budgeting — a Definite Help

Budgeting for families, of course, is no sure-fire method for keeping expenditures within income, because no matter how hard a family tries or how well spending is planned, unexpected expenditures constantly come up. But a budget does help! Families who live by them are able to manage their resources much more effectively. If your family will be alert to change and adjust its budgets to meet its needs, then your family budget can be a very worthwhile guide in your spending. It's no easy cure for "spenditis," but it is an indication of a financially concerned family.

Chapter 2

Family Financial Records

Adequate, accurate financial records are essential for proper family money management. Without having necessary financial information readily available for review, evaluation, and projection of the family's budget goals, it is impossible to carry through on a program of family budgeting. The accuracy of a variety of financial reports, especially a family's income tax return, is dependent upon adequate, accurate financial records. Even supplementary records, such as insurance records, inventory of assets, mortgage payment records, are also very important for family planning.

But while record keeping is so important, methods will vary considerably, depending on the information needed or desired. Records kept only for preparing income tax returns would include certain limited information. But a complete budget system for a family of six, where comparisons and evaluations of money earned and spent over the years is desired, will of necessity be much more elaborate. Supplementary record keeping will depend on the family's needs and desires and the amount of assets and liabilities.

Many of the methods suggested in this chapter will need to be modified to suit the needs of a particular family. The suggestions listed here are made in the hope that they may be adequate for most clergymen and their families. Family financial records should develop around the needs, abilities, and experiences of the family. The system should be simple and convenient, for a cumbersome system will soon discourage even the most ambitious family. A simple record keeping system can provide accurate, understandable information

16

when it is most needed. Some experimentation will soon show what can be handled most readily and what information will be most desirable. Any system ought to be changed when necessary in order to make it even more effective in providing desired information.

Of course, no matter how reliable or perfect your system, record keeping alone will not solve your money problems. It will perhaps reveal weaknesses in your spending plan. It will show you where the money comes from and where it goes. But it will not be a substitute for wise and intelligent use of your money. Records are only a resource, a guide, a help. They are not problem solvers, only problem revealers. In the final analysis, what you do with the information you get from your records will determine their usefulness to your family's money management program. Design your records properly, use them intelligently, and they will be a tremendous source of help toward a wise planning of your family's money uses.

Checking Accounts

Perhaps the most basic of all financial records is the family bankbook with its check stubs, bank statement, and cancelled checks. In fact, for most families this is about the sum total of their record keeping. But even this basic record can be quite confusing and inadequate for families unaccustomed to proper and accurate record keeping. While many of us may consider it unthinkable to be without a checking account, there are many families, perhaps some of them clergymen's families, who have no bank accounts at all and make all payments by cash.

For the clergyman's family, however, whose annual income in today's economy will be thousands of dollars, serious consideration should be given to the proper use of a checking account. The advantages far outweigh any objections, and actually the cost is small for the services available. The banker in your community will be glad to point out the obvious advantages of using a checking account.

For one thing, if you pay all your bills by check, you will have a complete record of all your expenditures. Your check stubs or your cancelled checks returned to you are your record of money spent. Deposit slips will indicate the source of funds.

A checking account also provides you with complete protection for your funds, while cash can be easily misappropriated when lost or stolen. Almost all bank deposits today are insured by the Federal Deposit Insurance Corporation; thus each depositor has insurance coverage up to $10,000 on his account. Of course, your money is there for you whenever you want it, but in the meantime it is safe.

Properly written or endorsed checks can be sent through the mails or carried in billfolds and purses with only the slightest possibility of misappropriation by forgery if lost or stolen. Furthermore, paying by check is a convenient and simple method for taking care of your obligations whether by mail or in person.

A very positive advantage to having a checking account is its usefulness in providing for a more intelligent family spending plan. Little or no family financial planning often results in impulsive buying, and using cash enhances the probabilities of overspending even more. While a checking account is no guarantee against improper or even impulsive buying and spending, it is a deterrent. Since a properly kept checkbook will show your account balance at all times, you may think twice before buying, knowing what your balance is. Furthermore, check writing takes more time and is more cumbersome than paying cash, thus is less likely to be done impulsively.

Check writing facilities are not free, and yet they are not expensive. Costs vary from one bank to another depending on the services provided. One bank charges $.03 for each check written, with a minimum monthly charge of $1.00 offset with a credit of $.15 for each $100.00 balance in your account (the lowest account balance for the month). Out-of-town checks included in deposits are charged to your account at $.05 each. A dime-a-time checking account is provided by another bank for those who write only a few checks each month. The only cost is $.10 for each check you write.

The procedures for having a checking account—opening a new account, using it, closing it out—will vary from one banking institution to another. It may be well to discuss the matter at several banks, for the bank which you choose should provide other services to meet your anticipated financial needs.

Selecting a bank is much like selecting a doctor or a grocery store or an insurance agent. You go where you will get the service you need at a cost you consider reasonable. With banks, as with most things, you will get no more than you pay for, and it is neither wise nor expedient to select a bank simply because it has the smallest monthly service charge.

A family which plans wisely will look for a family doctor who can take care of their physical needs, not only to make them well, but also to keep them well. While the cost for such services may be a consideration, few families shop around for the least expensive doctors. A well-qualified, helpful, considerate physician will be of greater concern than the cost. An insurance agent is chosen with similar care, for the prudent family manager will select the agent who can give qualified, intelligent, long-range planning to the family's insurance needs. While no one is anxious to pay more than necessary for insurance coverage, the insurance agent who takes an interest in the family's long-term needs will be preferred over the man who offers a quick bargain now and never gives any more help. The selection of a family attorney, as will be explained in a subsequent chapter, needs just as careful attention.

The selection of a bank should be made with equal care. A financial advisor can be extremely important over the years. Your bank should have officers and employees who are willing and capable of giving necessary advice and guidance to your family concerning its financial matters. Choose your bank with care, but remember that convenience of location and hours and reasonableness of service charges should not be the only considerations affecting your choice.

Checking Account Procedures

The mechanics of using a checking account may seem rather routine and simple to most of us. After all, what is involved except the writing of checks and the depositing of the monthly pay check? And we would have to agree, not much more is usually involved. But many times in the routineness of using a checking account we overlook some of the important details or incorrectly assume that what we have been doing all these years is correct. Perhaps some of the following suggestions and illustrations will help you to use your checking account and your bank to better advantage.

Opening a checking account usually involves no more than a brief conference with a secretary, although at more progressive and public-relations-minded banks a junior officer or even an administrative assistant may be assigned to open new accounts. Such institutions are aware of the importance of this initial contact and not only wish to create a favorable impression but also want to be certain that the new account is properly serviced from the beginning. But whoever the officer assigned to open the account, certain routine procedures are necessary.

The secretary or officer will fill in pertinent information on a new account card, make your initial deposit for you, and ask for your usual signature on a signature card for identification of the checks you write against your account. If this is a single account, only in your name, this will be all that is necessary. If you and your wife both intend to write checks on this particular account, then your wife's signature will also be required.

You should read the signature card carefully to be certain that the legal phraseology says what you want it to say. With a joint account you will probably prefer a statement that permits the survivor (yourself or your wife) to have whatever money is in the account upon the death of the other and will not want it included in the estate of the deceased. A joint account with right of survivorship is what you should insist on. Ask your banker or, if you wish, your attorney, for an explanation of the fine print on the signature card.

If these right-of-survivorship precautions are not considered, your wife could be left without any cash funds immediately available to her at your death. The bank would be required to "freeze" your account, and it might be several days before a judge would permit their use, pending an evaluation and inventory of your estate. Similar precautions should be exercised with your safety deposit box, since a box in your name only will be sealed at your death by your banker and opened only by action of the court. Since laws vary from state to state, it is important for you to inquire about these matters in the place where you live.

By far the majority of American families do have joint checking accounts. Such an arrangement is more convenient (and cheaper, too) for the family's banking procedures and its financial record keeping, and it fosters the spirit of family cooperation which is so important in money matters. Statistics are unavailable, but estimates would surely indicate that there are more family quarrels over finances than over any other single matter. A joint account won't solve these problems, but it may be conducive to greater harmony and understanding. When husband and wife have separate accounts there can be a selfish tendency to declare that "what's in my account is mine!" Christian families will respond in the spirit of family solidarity and unity in any areas of life where they can. Perhaps a joint account is one small way of encouraging a more wholesome attitude toward the family's finances.

When you have finally made these various arrangements for opening a checking account, including the necessary signatures, you will receive a supply of checks and deposit slips along with instructions for using your account.

Making Deposits

Clergymen, among others, should be properly informed about making deposits as well as about cashing and writing checks. Perhaps some of the following ideas will be helpful.

A check that is to be deposited must first be properly endorsed, "Pay to the Order of the First State Bank of Anywhere, For Deposit Only" with your name written exactly as it appears on the check. While "For Deposit Only" or similar notations may have gotten you by in the past, the above endorsement is preferred, especially if you deposit checks by mail. That kind of endorsement specifically designates the person or institution which will be transferring its funds to you or your account in receipt of your check.

A simple or blank endorsement of your name across the back of a check is generally sufficient when you are personally cashing a check made out to you, but even so, a "Pay to the Order of . . . " provides considerably more protection and assurance that the proper person receives the check. A check made out to "Cash" at your bank is insufficient, although it can get money for you. A "Bearer" check is also often inadequate or unsafe, although it, too, can be cashed. And a check left blank, which has been signed by you but has neither payee nor amount written in, is an invitation to misappropriation!

Deposit slips should give all the necessary information about the checks or cash you are placing in your account. List the silver and currency, and then each check separately. Many banks prefer that you list not only the drawer's name from each check on the deposit slip, but that you also list the cashing bank's location (if out of town) and its identification number. This code number, assigned to each bank by the American Bankers Association, is usually located in the upper right corner or lower left corner of the check and is used to identify the bank where the drawer's funds are located. Take a look at any check and you'll notice this number—a hyphenated number above a line with another number below it. Use the top number to identify each of the checks you deposit.

When you have completed your deposit, be sure to keep a copy of your deposit slip on hand so you will know what funds were deposited, how much they totaled, and where they came from.

Writing Checks

You have probably written hundreds of checks in your lifetime, and there seems little reason to tell you how to do it now. But your banker could likely cite many instances of checks that have been written improperly even though they were cashed and otherwise cleared through the banking processes.

A correctly written check (using ink or ball-point pen or typewriter, but definitely not a pencil) will include various procedures. Each check will be numbered consecutively. The correct current date will be inserted. The payee's name will be written out in full beginning as far to the left as possible on the "Pay to the Order of . . . " line. The name will be legible and correctly written without Mr. or Dr. or Mrs. or other prefatory title. The whole line will be filled all the way to the dollar sign with a straight line if the name does not fill the space. Blank spaces are temptations for unscrupulous persons who come into possession of signed checks. Unauthorized altering of names or numbers by adding or changing letters and numbers can be done. While checks are protected against erasures, expertly made additions where no erasures are involved are easy to make and difficult to detect.

And the same precautions should be exercised in writing the rest of the check. Numerical figures should touch up against the dollar sign, and the amount written out in full in the next line should likewise fill in the entire space either with words or a line. The word "and" written at an angle helps prevent tampering. Your signature should be the same as appears on your signature card.

Should it be necessary to stop payment on a check, you may do so with a special request to your bank. Thus, if a check is lost or stolen, or you have reason to change your mind about a payment made by check because it is incorrect or you are dissatisfied with the merchandise or service, or for any number of reasons, you can ask your bank not to honor that check for payment. They will do so if your request is made soon enough and the check has not already cleared your account. This protects you from your own errors as well as the possible unscrupulous actions of others. The service costs a minimum amount.

Other Types of Cash

Besides checks and currency, there are other types of paper which circulate in the business world in the place of cash and are in fact used just like cash. Clergymen ought to be at least familiar with the terminology.

"Cashier's Check—A cashier's check is a bank's check drawn by its cashier on itself. Cashier's checks are used in the payment of the expenses and liabilities of a bank and are issued to depositors who may wish to purchase them. When a person wishes to make a payment where his own check may not be acceptable, he may purchase a cashier's check and use it."[1] Payment is assured because the cashier's check is a direct liability of the bank.

Certified Check—A certified check is a depositor's check upon the face of which a bank officer has written "accepted" or "certified," together with his signature and the date. "The amount of the check is deducted at once from the depositor's account in the bank, and thereafter the certified check is a liability of the bank to the holder.

"Travelers' Checks—Travelers' checks are checks issued by a bank, bankers' association, or express company, all in even denominations, for the convenience of a traveler who is the purchaser. Each check carries a specimen of the signature of the purchaser. When the purchaser desires to cash one of the checks he identifies himself by countersigning the check to match the specimen of his signature. Travelers' checks are accepted generally by hotels and banks.

"Express and Postal Money Orders—An express money order is an order (sight draft) of an express company payable at any one of its branches. It is used for the same purpose as a check. One important

---

[1]George A. MacFarland, Robert D. Ayars, Willard E. Stone, *Accounting Fundamentals,* third edition (Copyright © 1957 McGraw-Hill Book Company, Inc., New York), pp. 171-172. Used by permission of McGraw-Hill Book Company.

use is to remit cash for a C.O.D. shipment sent by express. A postal money order is an order (sight draft) issued by one postmaster on another but payable on identification at any post office."[2]

"Bank Draft—A bank draft is a check drawn by one bank against funds deposited to its account in another bank. Bank drafts are commonly purchased for making remittances to distant places where a bank check is more acceptable than an individual's check or where the payee of the check has requested that exchange be provided on the town or city where his place of business is located. They may also be purchased for use in international transactions with the draft issued in the currency of the foreign country."[3] Or bank drafts may be purchased in the same way as cashier's checks by persons who want to use them for making payments where their personal check may not be acceptable.

"Traveler's Letter of Credit—A traveler's letter of credit is a letter of credit issued by a bank to a customer preparing for an extended trip. The customer pays for the letter of credit and the bank issues the letter for a specified period of time in the amount purchased. The bank furnishes a list of correspondent banks where drafts drawn against the letter of credit will be honored. The bank also identifies the customer by exhibiting a specimen signature of the purchaser on the folder enclosing the list of correspondent banks. The purchaser may go to any bank listed, draw a draft against the letter of credit, and receive credit. Each bank that honors a draft endorses on the letter of credit the date a payment was honored, the name of the honoring bank, and the amount drawn against the letter of credit."[3]

Banking Services

Banking services vary considerably from one institution to another. One bank which lists thirty services[4] "tailored to fit your needs" includes: low-cost checking accounts, regular checking accounts, busi-

---

[2]*Ibid.*
[3]Kenneth E. Broin, assistant vice-president, First National Bank, Minneapolis, Minn.
[4]Another bank lists fifty-two services!

ness checking accounts, regular savings accounts, student savings accounts, automatic savings, Christmas club savings, commercial loans, home improvement loans, farm mortgage loans, farm equipment loans, farm operating loans, collateral loans, automobile loans, signature loans, boat loans, appliance loans, personal loans, certificate of deposit, foreign remittances, bank by mail, travelers' checks, night deposit, money orders, U.S. Savings Bonds, F.H.A. loans, vacation loans, safe deposit boxes, payment of telephone, gas, and Blue Cross bills—with "no request too small, no requirement too large." The convenience is yours at little cost.

As an added convenience, you may want your church treasurer to deposit your salary check for you each month. Of course, this won't cost you anything, and you will be free of any concern for doing it yourself. In fact, if you really don't want to be bothered with a lot of the details of your own personal finances, someone else can do most of it for you. Ask your banker for information.

Bank Statement Reconciliation

If you are going to keep a dependable record of your financial transactions, it will be necessary for you to keep an accurate record of your deposits and checks. A reconciliation of your own checkbook to the monthly bank statement will then be necessary. This is required because the balance on the bank statement you receive is seldom the same as your checkbook balance. Service charges, deposits you made after the bank statement was mailed to you, and checks you have written but which have not yet been cashed, or if they have, have not cleared through the bank (outstanding checks), will all account for the difference.

The following procedures are suggested to assure inclusion in your checkbook of all charges made against your account as well as to be certain of the accuracy of your checkbook stubs. You can assume that the bank statement is accurate.

Use two columns. At the top of the first column show your checkbook balance; at the top of the second column show the balance of your bank statement. Subtract from the checkbook balance in the first column the service charges made by the bank on your account which do not yet appear in your checkbook. Subtract or add any other charges or credits applied against your account by the bank. Be sure to record all such charges and credits in your checkbook too. The total in this column then is your corrected checkbook balance.

Now list and total in the second column all your outstanding checks, that is, those which do not show on the bank statement but which you have written and deducted in your checkbook. Subtract this total from the bank statement balance at the top of this column. Next, determine which deposits you have recently made which do not appear on your bank statement. Add these to the sub-total in column two. This is your adjusted bank account balance.

Now your adjusted bank statement and corrected checkbook balance should be equal. If so, all is well. If not, recheck the arithmetic in your checkbook and the calculations of your reconciliation. Chances are *you* have made the error somewhere, not the bank, and you will probably soon find the difference.

Preparing a bank reconciliation such as this will give you the control you need over your checking account and also provide you with the accuracy necessary to let you know exactly where you are cash-wise at any given moment.

Financial Record Keeping in Your Home

A good record keeping system may well be the key to successful management of your money. In a sense it becomes the cornerstone of your family's entire spending plan. Of course, there are many things that must be done in family money management besides record keeping, but all the other plans are rather ineffective if your system for keeping track of income and expenses is inadequate. Budget comparisons are impossible, and you cannot possibly know how much you have spent, where the money has gone, how accurate your spending plan really is, and what changes you need to make in order to bring your spending in line with the realities of your income if you do not have an effective record keeping system.

Your checkbook record is insufficient for keeping track of all your income and expenses. While you may regularly deposit your pay check, you will probably just pocket the baptismal and wedding honorariums you occasionally receive. Large cash gifts or unusual receipts may also be deposited, but the tendency will be for you to ignore the several small fees you may receive from time to time. Needless to say, an accounting must also be made of these, if for no other purpose than for your income tax return. Since these fees may be a considerable amount for some clergymen, they must be considered in the development of a spending plan. Record keeping beyond your checkbook is essential for any kind of intelligent analysis of what is happening to your finances.

What is true for your income is equally true for your expenses. Of course, your checkbook does provide a chronological listing of all checks written, and this same record will be a listing of all your expenses if you pay everything by check. But if you pay some items with cash, you have no record of those items on your check stubs. And besides, correlating all those various payments for your tax return or other reports may not be so simple. A separate systematic listing can be very valuable.

Numerous systems have been proposed, and another one, such as described here, may add little to the cumulative information on family record keeping. In fact, each family must design the system that is best for its own use. But use what you can from the various sources available, including this one, in order to develop your own system geared to your own needs.

Designing the system best for your family begins with a clear understanding of the kind of information you want to get from your records. Elaborate systems may provide a wealth of statistics, but simple systems can often give you all you really need for your family's planning. And as you begin to use your records, you will of course revise, delete, and add so that whatever statistics or records you need will soon be available to you with the least amount of effort.

If you have already developed a spending plan in your previous budget preparations, as described in the previous chapter, you may very well use that same outline of items; at least your spending plan and your record keeping system ought to be similar. This will be important when you begin making comparisons between your budget plan and what you actually spend. A system such as that illustrated on the following pages may prove helpful to your family.

Monthly Analysis of Financial Records

Once you have developed a satisfactory record keeping system and used it for a while, you can begin to make comparisons and analyses. While it is extremely difficult to make any kind of systematic study of your finances if you have no more than a confusing assortment of check stubs, even your newly created financial records have not proved their ultimate worth until you begin to evaluate what is going on. Hopefully you have developed a system that makes worthwhile comparative evaluations practical and even possible.

Your first evaluation will be to check the nearness of your actual income and expenses for the past month with your estimated earning and spending plan. If you have developed the forms suggested in this chapter, then it is a simple matter to fill in the blanks and compare, item by item, just how well you have done. Not every comparison, of course, will show your expenses and your estimates as exactly equal. In fact, none of your actual expenses may be the same as what you estimated, except for your regular monthly payments on notes, insurance, and the like. But if your initial guesses were at all realistic, the two columns should be relatively similar.

You may not need to be concerned with significant differences after only the first month of record keeping. But if differences continue in subsequent months within the same expense categories, then some adjustments in your spending plan need to be made.

DAILY SPENDING RECORD   MONTH OF_____

Item* Day	Food	Home operations	Transportation	Recreation	Personal care	Gifts	Miscellaneous			Comments
1										
2										
3										
etc.										
31										
Total Mo. Exp.**										

* To simplify the extension of columns on this record, payments which are made infrequently—not more than once a month—may be noted directly on the Monthly Spending Record Summary rather than on this daily report.

** Totals of each column should be copied onto the Monthly Spending Record Summary form at the end of each month.

MONTHLY SPENDING RECORD SUMMARY   YEAR_____

Item	Month _____		Month _____		Month _____	
	Plan	Actual	Plan	Actual	Plan	
Income—						
Expenses—						

If your estimated expenses are regularly more than you actually spend (the reverse is more likely) and you are able to build up your cash balances each month, then you are very fortunate. You may want to give some thought to investing these funds or setting aside savings rather than purposely increasing your expenses.

On the other hand, if your actual expenses consistently exceed your estimated spending plan (as well as your income), then you may be heading for some trouble. But the possibilities of locating the problem and doing something about it are far greater when you are using a dependable record keeping system than if you have to wade through scribbled notations on bank stubs.

To review your plan, go back to your record, month by month, and search out those areas where you are spending more than you originally thought you would. Examine them closely. Is there any way in which these expenditures can be reduced? Or are there other items which can be reduced? Can you eliminate some non-essentials? Have you overcommitted yourself with debts? If so, what can you do about it? Are your tastes too high? Have you bought unnecessary items? Have you overpaid?

Perhaps additional sources of income are needed if you are convinced you have cut your expenses to the bone. Investigate some possibilities that will not interfere with your regular church responsibilities. As a last choice, and definitely not a very good one, consider a short-term bank loan to tide you over. But be sure you have a good plan in mind that will eventually cut expenses and pay off the loan, because otherwise even your banker may not be too anxious to help you.

There are several other items which you may want to consider from time to time as you are reviewing your financial records. For instance, you are obviously interested in saving as much as you can. If 10% of your take-home pay for savings seems reasonable to you, then try it when you set up your spending plan. If you have simply taken a random amount for savings initially, compare it to your salary now. Can you improve the percentage?

For many people the payment of rent or a mortgage is the largest single monthly payment they make and perhaps the most inevitable. For clergymen who have a parsonage furnished, this is no problem. But if you are one of the growing fortunate few clergymen who receive a house allowance, what percentage of your total salary (including house allowance) is used for your rent or mortgage plus utilities and maintenance? For tax purposes the house allowance is significant, but for determining the amount you spend on rent or mortgage payments it is probably not too meaningful.

As will be explained in a subsequent chapter, professional advice to potential home buyers often suggests that you can afford to spend no more than one-fourth of your total take-home pay for all your housing expenses. How do you compare?

What percentage of your income do you spend on insurance each year (or each month, if you divide your annual premium into monthly payments—a more expensive procedure, by the way)? Perhaps your insurance agent needs to go over your coverage with you to suggest improvements in your present plan.

There are, of course, other evaluations which you can easily make. Determine the ones which are most helpful to you, and then after a study of them, make such adjustments in your plan as seem necessary for your evaluations.

Keeping Records for Tax Purposes

The clergyman who fails to keep adequate records to support his income tax calculations is asking for trouble. Over and over again Internal Revenue Service officials require taxpayers to substantiate their claims for deductions and exclusions. You must keep track of certain basic items in order to satisfy the request of Revenue agents.

While you may insist that your records have never been checked, and besides your income is so small as to be a waste of time for anyone to check into, nevertheless the law requires that you be able to substantiate the amounts inserted on your return. Some day your return may be audited, and then for sure you must have the necessary information readily available. In the meantime, the record keeping required will assist you in keeping properly informed about your finances.

Clergymen have a few more allowable deductions and exclusions than most people. They must be especially careful to maintain a satisfactory set of records of receipts and expenses if they expect to take advantage of the many liberal provisions of the tax regulations peculiarly available to them.

Briefly, you should keep a running record of your car expenses (gas, oil, repairs, insurance, tires, business-use mileage, etc.), contributions to your church and other charitable organizations, taxes (sales, property, etc.), interest you pay on loans and mortgages, all medical expenses and drugs, professional expenses (books, supplies, etc.).

If you receive a house allowance, you should keep careful records of all expenses applicable to reducing this allowance for exclusion from income, items such as house or rent payments, utilities, repairs, maintenance, insurance, etc. As will be more fully explained later, your house allowance is excludable from taxable income only to the extent to which you use it to purchase, provide, or maintain a home.

A simple form of a few columns—date, to whom paid, amount, and various categories—will be enough record keeping, together with pertinent notes, for these various tax deductions and exclusion items, if this is all the record keeping you intend to do. At the end of the year add up the columns for each category and you have the information you need for your return.

Inventory of Household Goods Records

In addition to the records listed thus far, there are several other records and schedules which may be helpful. Of course, records can be kept for almost anything, but some rather essential information would be easily available if the following particular records were kept accurately, in addition to the monthly spending plan schedules.

There are several good reasons why a family should keep an up-to-date list and valuation of its household goods. Perhaps the most obvious reason is that an intelligent valuation can then be made for household insurance coverage or for any other valuation or appraisal required. Furthermore, if the inventory list is kept in a safe place, it will be very useful in case of fire or other major catastrophe. Some kind of listing will certainly be needed in such an event. Unfortunately very few families have such an inventory, and if those without such a record are ever required to list their furniture and clothing and their value, they would be hard put to determine an accurate valuation.

Here again, a simple form is sufficient and provides all the necessary information. The following is suggested:

INVENTORY OF HOUSEHOLD GOODS

Item	Date purchased	From whom purchased	Cost	Expected life	Appraised value*

*An annual reappraisal is desirable.

Then, if, due to a calamity, it should ever be necessary to replace items, the replacement value will most likely be used to determine the payments received, and such value, if you have a record, is likely to be greater than if there are no records.

Appraisal calculations are usually an intelligent guess by someone familiar with the item in question, someone able to determine the item's change in value due to aging, obsolescence, usefulness, etc. It may be sufficient for the ordinary family, not expert in appraising, to determine for its own purposes of appraisal the expected useful years of an item, especially furniture and appliances (Internal Revenue Service lists may be available for this), and then annually reduce the cost price by this percentage. A washing machine, for instance, is simply worth more now than it will be five years later. But how valuable is it now and how valuable will it be five years from now? How much longer will it be serviceable? How much would it cost to replace the machine with one of equal dependability and quality? These are the kinds of things to consider in making appraisals.

An on-going inventory record of current values of all the things you possess will provide valuable information at any time.

Insurance Records

Insurance will be discussed at considerable length in another chapter and a suggested form for listing insurance policies and coverages of all types is illustrated there. Here it is sufficient to emphasize that your policies and such a record of your policies should also be kept in a safe place. Furthermore, some individual outside of the family circle ought to know where your insurance listing is kept. This becomes particularly important at a time of death or disaster or other crises when the insured may not be available and insurance coverage must be ascertained as quickly as possible.

Note Payment Record

The clergyman's family which owes other people money on small loans, installment purchases, a mortgage, or for any other reason, ought to keep adequate records on forms similar to those illustrated below for each loan.

NOTE PAYMENT RECORD

Amount_____ Payee_____

Date of note_____ Due date_____ Rate_____

Terms_____

Date	Amount paid	Interest	Principal	Balance

Home Purchase and Maintenance Records

Few home owners realize the importance of accurate, detailed records for all expenses of purchasing and maintaining a home. If for no other reason than to determine a profit or loss on the sale of your home for income tax purposes, accurate records must be kept. The original cost of your house and all the major improvements must be known. Even though present income tax regulations do not require the payment of a tax when you sell your home at a profit and purchase another residence within twelve months (a loss is not deductible in any case), your records must be available to substantiate your claims.

But as you buy and sell homes you may not purchase another home within the prescribed time limit, or you may simply sell your last home, move into an apartment, and never again intend to buy another house. Then a tax must be paid on any accumulated profits you have enjoyed over the years. Accurate, detailed records are essential if this information is going to be readily available.

There may also come a time when you wish to rent your home. Then you must have accurate records of your initial costs and of all improvements so that depreciation, other expenses, a rate of return on your investment, and any profits received can be calculated. Or you may use a room or two for office space. If so, you are entitled to certain deductions from your taxable income. Accurate record keeping is necessary to determine the exact amount.

These records are also important in substantiating the full use of any house allowances received. Any amounts of your house allowance which are unexpended at the end of the year must be included in your taxable income. It becomes important, therefore, to keep accurate records so that you will be able to account for and thus deduct all proper expenses and take complete advantage of this generous provision. Items for which you may expend your house allowance include: down payment for the property, mortgage installment payments, legal fees in acquiring the property, bank fees paid to obtain the mortgage, fees for searching title, interest paid on the mortgage, real estate taxes, personal property taxes paid on the home (if any), assessments or levies against the property for special purposes (e.g. streets, sewers, etc.), fire and home liability insurance premiums, utilities, repairs, home furnishings. If the total of all these amounts exceeds the allowance, then you pay no income tax on any portion of it (you cannot deduct from income expenditures of these items in excess of the allowance). But if you cannot substantiate with accurate records the expenditure of the entire allowance, then you must pay income tax on any excess unused allowance. Additional information on this topic for home-owning clergymen is presented in chapter five.

The type of information which is important to have is suggested in the following illustrated record and includes all details related to such things as repairing or replacing a roof, painting, plumbing repairs, the addition of a room, papering, remodeling, added electrical wiring, fencing, landscaping, and so forth. A record of most of these items will also be necessary for income tax purposes, but a complete record will also be extremely valuable for future appraisals, listing of improvements for prospective purchasers, establishing a cost basis for charitable gifts tax valuation, and other purposes. Your records are valuable. Keep them accurate and up-to-date.

HOME PURCHASE AND MAINTENANCE RECORD

Deed number_____Recorded at_____Vol._____Page_____

Location of deed_____

Brief description of lot location_____

_____

Lot (and house) purchased from_____

Builder's name & address_____

Appraised value at time of purchase_____Date_____

Assessed value for tax purposes_____Annual taxes_____

Insurance coverage by_____Type of policy_____

_____Amount of policy_____Due date for premiums

Cost information:

    Price of lot _____

    Cost of house _____

    Closing costs _____

    Other costs _____

    Total _____

    Down payment _____ First mortgage _____

    Monthly payment _____ Monthly due date _____

    Terms: Years _____ Rate _____

    Mortgagee _____

CAPITAL IMPROVEMENTS RECORD

Date	Description	Cost	Work by	Financing

REPAIRS AND MINOR IMPROVEMENTS

Date	Description	Cost	Work by

UTILITY EXPENSE RECORD

	J	F	M	A	M	J	J	A	S	O	N	D
Heat												
Water												
Electricity												
Others												

SAVINGS RECORD

	Date	Emergency fund Bank_____	Future security Bank_____	Dream fund Bank_____	Total
Balance					
Deposit/Interest					
Balance					
Deposit/Interest					
etc.					

(The following four forms are adapted from *Personal Money Management*, First National Bank of Minneapolis, Minn.)

STOCKS RECORD

Company	Certificate No.	Date of Purchase	Number of shares	Price per share	Buying expense	Total cost	Date sold	Number of shares	Price per share	Selling expense	Amount received	Profit or loss

DIVIDEND INCOME RECORD

Company	Date	Amount	Date	Amount	Date	Amount	Date	Amount	Total for year

BONDS RECORD

Bond	Serial No.	Denomination	Date purchased	Price	Accrued interest	Commission	Cost	Date sold or redeemed	Price	Accrued interest	Commission	Amount received	Profit or loss

INTEREST INCOME RECORD

Date	Source	Amount

And finally, for the family that is eager to know what its financial status would be if something should happen to its salary earning capacity, the form on the next page may be useful.

Filing Your Records

The accumulation of all this information in an easy-to-find place and in a logical sequence is also important. Separate file folders containing pertinent information on insurance policies, notes, house costs, etc. are easy to use. A three-ring binder containing all the necessary schedules for your records with explicit instructions to your wife on what to do and whom to contact for various matters can also be extremely useful. Where possible, a fireproof box or safe should be used for safekeeping of important, irreplaceable records and instructions. But whatever procedure for filing you use, be certain that it is accurate, up-to-date, logically arranged, and familiar to your wife or any other person who may need to know some day about your affairs.

ESTATE PLANNING[5]

Source of money	Cash for last expenses, mortgages, emergency		Monthly family income		
	Amount	Use for	$ a month for ___yrs. 19___ to 19___	$ a month for ___yrs. 19___ to 19___	$ a month for ___yrs. 19___ to 19___
Social Sec.					
Life Ins.					
Life Ins.					
Life Ins.					
Investment					
Other					
Total					

Husband's will_____dated_____where kept_____

Wife's will_____dated_____where kept_____

Name, address, and phone number of lawyer_____

Safe deposit box and key_____where kept_____

Date this estimate calculated_____

---

[5]Adapted from *The Christian Family and Money Management,* Commission on Stewardship, Lutheran Laymen's Movement for Stewardship, Lutheran Church in America, New York, and the Commission on Stewardship and Benevolence of the National Council of Churches of Christ in the U.S.A.

Chapter 3

Installment Buying

"Credit has made America!" is a timeworn cliche descriptive of the tremendous significance credit buying has had on the American economy. Without credit our economy and our standard of living would likely never have become what it is today. Almost every family in America makes regular, monthly installment payments of one kind or another on a home mortgage, a car, appliances, a vacation trip, jewelry, stock purchases, and a wide assortment of other items, services, and conveniences. In short, credit is a vital part of the "American way of life."

However, credit buying on the installment plan can be an expensive business. Too often the extra costs are overlooked or ignored, or at least smoothed over by the soothing balm of no down payments, low monthly payments, "discount" rates of interest! The unsuspecting and uninformed purchaser will pay much more than the agreed-on-price by the time he pays off the installment contract in full.

Unsuspecting clergymen are caught in this squeeze, too. Often, when they are overly ambitious to have certain "comforts of life," they can be caught in a web of monthly payments that will virtually choke their finances to death. However, with careful spending, prudent borrowing, a bit of patience, and some "business spirit," even a minister can "keep up with the Joneses"—at least to some extent!

Of course, buying for cash is never a bad habit. This does not mean avoiding charge accounts, but it does mean avoiding exorbitant charges and interest rates attached to installment buying on month-by-month payment plans. Ordinary thirty-day charge accounts are fine, useful, and practical, so long as a service charge or some other additional cost is not added for the credit service. Paying by cash ordinarily means making one lump-sum payment at the time of purchase, or by the end of the month, or within the next thirty days.

However, buying large items for cash is ordinarily impossible without some advance planning of needs and a systematic method of saving. It may also mean putting off some purchases for a while. But if you can save the money first, then pay cash for your purchases, you will get more for your money.

The family which insists on buying on installments anyway—and there is nothing wrong with doing so—ought to know what is involved and take advantage of some cash-saving possibilities.

For instance, the usual 4% car loan, which may also be quoted at a "$4 per hundred" rate, is really not a 4% loan after all, for in effect more than 4% is actually paid. Under such a loan, the amount repaid will include not only the amount borrowed, but $4 for each hundred dollars of the total loan for each year until the loan is paid in full. On a $2,500, 36-month loan, for instance, this could mean $300 in interest costs alone, or an effective rate of 7.7%, almost double the 4%!

The following formula may be of interest to you for calculating the effective rate at which you are paying interest on an installment loan:

$$R = \frac{2\,Ni}{P\,(n+1)}$$

Where: R = the effective interest rate (in decimal form)
N = the number of payment periods in a year
i = actual interest charges (in dollars)
P = net amount of the loan
n = number of payments to be made

Substituting the data in the foregoing illustration for the symbols in the formula, then, we get the following:

$$R = \frac{2 \times 12 \times 300}{2500\,(36+1)} = \frac{7200}{92500} = .077$$

(an effective rate of interest for this loan of slightly more than 7.7%).

Arrange with your banker for a 6% loan, though, with interest cal-culated on the outstanding balance of the loan, and you pay much less interest. A $2,500 loan over a 36-month period under this arrange-ment would involve only $238.16 in interest paid out. If you were ever fortunate enough to get a 4% loan, interest on the outstanding balance, you would pay only $157.16 in interest costs on a 36-month $2,500 loan!

Or a twelve-month, short-term installment loan of $1,000 at a quoted rate of $6 per hundred would be paid off at $88.33 a month ($1,000 times 6% divided by 12) with a total interest cost of $60; but a regular 6% bank loan would be paid off at $86.05 a month for a total interest cost of $32.84, since interest would be computed on the outstanding balance each month—a savings of $27.16!

And the same thing would be true for any other installment buy-ing, except that with major appliances various other charges plus the interest are added to the original price, thus raising the total costs even more.

Typical Credit Charges[1]

If charges are based on the beginning amount owed and are in-cluded in the 12 equal monthly installments:

If charged:	*Simple annual rate is:*
$4 per $100 or 4% per year	7.4%
$6 per $100 or 6% per year	11.1%
$8 per $100 or 8% per year	14.8%
$10 per $100 or 10% per year	18.5%
1% per month	22.2%

If charged only on *unpaid amount owed:*

If charged:	*Simple annual rate is:*
¾ of 1% per month on unpaid balance	9%
5/6 of 1% per month on unpaid balance	10%

---

[1]*Consumer's Quick Credit Guide,* United States Government Printing Office, 1964, 0-728-434.

1% per month on unpaid balance 12%
1¼% per month on unpaid balance 15%
1½% per month on unpaid balance 18%
2½% per month on unpaid balance 30%

The advantages of using consumer credit for installment buying may be summarized as follows:[2]

1. It lets you buy things you want or need if you do not have the ready cash available.

2. It helps you to time your expenditures better and take advantage of such opportunities as bargain prices.

3. It allows you to keep available money for other uses and as an emergency reserve.

4. It may prevent disturbing permanent investments for temporary needs for cash.

5. And it may help you to get things that you cannot save for. If your income seems to slip away with little to show for it, you may need the discipline of regular payments.

The disadvantages of installment buying would include:

1. You risk being unable to make payments and having the lender repossess the item you are buying.

2. If you have overcommitted yourself in installment payments, you may find it difficult to meet payments on other debts.

3. You may be encouraged to use installment credit without fully checking your needs and your repayment ability. The point is not how much you can borrow but how well you can pay it back.

4. You usually pay more by using consumer credit than by paying cash.

---

[2]United States Department of Agriculture, Farmer's Bulletin No. 2135.

Of course, banks are eager to lend money to dependable people; this is one way banks make money. Ministers who have a good relationship with the banker in their area will have little difficulty in arranging for the most effective loans and, in fact, ought to talk with their banker before purchasing merchandise on time. Good credit ratings, a financial statement, and a sensible plan for repayment impress bankers. In the purchase of large items, the bank may insist on collateral, that is, some property, usually the new item being purchased, as protection in case you can't make the required payments. But the terms of a bank note can usually be arranged to suit the convenience of the borrower.

Obviously, then, credit is a means to achieving an objective. It enables a person to buy or invest when he does not have enough cash for the purpose. But it must be used intelligently and with a knowledge of all the risks involved. In the past some clergymen have abused the privilege, and in some people's minds the association continues for all clergymen. Careful inquiry and an intelligent understanding of what is involved will help avoid the pitfalls of consumer credit buying. Use credit wisely and intelligently, and it can help you attain those goals you so earnestly desire.

Chapter 4

Insurance

Life Insurance

Insurance is available for many different purposes. Indeed, coverage can actually be secured for almost any kind of desired protection —for a price. And perhaps the most common type of coverage is life insurance.

Indeed life insurance is a tremendously large business in America today. More Americans than ever before have become insurance conscious, and they are spending increasingly more every year for all sorts of coverages and protection.

Clergymen, like other heads-of-households, are eager to provide protection for their families in case anything should happen to them. Life insurance assures a man of that kind of protection for his survivors. It can also help a family to save money for retirement, for children's education, or for any other purpose, all the while providing life insurance coverage for the father. Its primary function is protection for the family should anything happen to the wage earner.

Insurance of any type is simply the collective action of a group of people contributing to a common fund an amount sufficient to compensate those few in the group who may suffer an actual loss. Forerunners of many of today's reputable insurance companies were simply a group of men who agreed to contribute a specific annual sum to a fund that would be used as a contribution to the family of anyone in the group in case of an accident or death, or for whatever purpose the fund was established. The arrangement minimized the effect of the loss suffered by any member of the group.

Life insurance developed from the same kind of concern. But now the loss was suffered by someone other than the person who was insured, and the event insured against, the death of the person, was sure to occur. The time of the event was the only thing uncertain about the arrangement. Insurance companies then developed mortality tables based on actual statistics of deaths in a given number of previous years in order to develop a systematic method for computing an individual's contribution to the common fund. On the basis of such tables (periodically revised) insurance companies are able to set premiums which when paid will accumulate up to the agreed-upon settlement amount if the insured lives as long as the tables say he should. Obviously, the calculations are based on averages such that the total premium accumulations, plus earnings on those premiums, are supposed to equal the total policy face values. Spread out among many policyholders, the early and late deaths will average out the statistics and do indeed prove the validity of the mortality estimates. Of course, some policyholders must pay more, others pay less, for the same protection.

In return, then, for the premiums you pay based on the mortality table calculations, the insurance company agrees to pay to you or your survivor, depending upon the terms of your policy, a specific sum. The amount paid is usually the face amount of the policy plus accumulated dividends and interest earnings less policy loans. The amount is paid to you at a certain age if your policy so stipulates or to your survivors if payment is due at your death. The kind of settlement your policy calls for will depend upon the kind of insurance you purchased and the various provisions of your policy.

But whatever kind you do decide upon, and the differences will be explained later, a policyholder's needs do change as he grows older and as his responsibilities increase or decrease. The man with a growing family needs protection for his wife and young children, while the man whose children are grown needs less protection for his wife than he did for a larger family. When the older man dies his widow's needs can be met with a far lesser amount than those of the widow with minor children. When children have completed college, their father's insurance needs will also differ from the time when they were younger. When the home mortgage is paid off, or virtually paid off, a man's life insurance needs change again. Savings for retirement will require one type of insurance; maximum coverage for the young family requires something else.

Before you make a decision to buy life insurance or increase or change your present coverage, you should be familiar with the various types of coverage which are available and with what each can do for you. Depending on your age, your family, your responsibilities, and your resources, you can choose from a variety of coverages available from almost any insurance company.

There are four basic kinds of life insurance policies: term, straight life (also called ordinary life or whole life), limited payment life, and endowment. Other kinds of insurance are simply variations of these or combinations or with special features. Costs vary, of course, depending upon the age of the insured, the coverage desired, the risks involved, the type of policy requested. While costs vary according to type, the older a person becomes, the greater the cost for any particular type of coverage. Once the premium has been set, however, whatever your age, it stays the same as long as the coverage is not altered.

A clergyman, like any other family head, will be interested in getting the greatest amount of coverage and protection for the least amount of cost. For instance, at age 30, $150 a year will buy about $16,200 of term insurance (to age 65), $8,000 of ordinary life, $5,500 of 20-year payment, and $3,400 of 20-year endowment.

These four types of insurance policies are succinctly described in a government publication as follows:[1]

Term Insurance offers the lowest cost protection for a period of time. It covers a certain number of years—usually 1, 5, or 10. Payment is made by the company if the insured dies during that time. If death

---

[1] *Understanding Life Insurance for the Family*, United States Department of Agriculture, December, 1964, pp. 4-5.

does not occur during this time, protection ends unless a new policy is taken out.

You may want to select a term insurance policy with a "renewable clause." This means you can renew your policy without another medical examination.

Some companies will not renew term policies after you are 50 or 60 years of age. Of course, you are likely to have fewer dependents at this age. Your life insurance needs are less.

You may also want to choose a term insurance policy with a "convertible clause." This permits you to change it later to some form of permanent life insurance such as straight life, if you wish.

Term insurance has no "cash" or loan value. You cannot borrow against it.

Straight Life Insurance is often called ordinary or whole life. The face value of the policy is paid only when the insured person dies. (Or if the policy so states, at an agreed upon age, usually age 96.) The premium rate is higher than the rate on a term policy, is lower than the rate on any other permanent policy, depends on your age at the time you buy your policy, and stays the same each year.

This policy builds a *cash value*. The value increases the longer the policy is kept. So, this policy builds up a loan value.

You may borrow against this value while continuing your insurance. Should you decide to give up the policy, you can take the cash in a lump sum, as income, or as paid-up insurance. The cash value is based on the number of years you have been paying.

If the insured person dies, the beneficiary is paid the face value (plus accumulated dividends if the insurance is with a mutual company). If there is a loan at the time of death, the money borrowed will be subtracted from the face value of the policy. The beneficiary will receive what is left.

Limited Payment Life Policies are different from straight life in several ways:

First, premiums are paid a limited number of years—10, 20, or 30.

Or you may pay premiums until you reach a certain age, usually 60 or 65 years.

Second, your annual premium rate is higher than for straight life. The reason is that you pay premiums only a certain number of years.

Third, the cash value of your policy increases faster since the premiums are higher.

Higher premium types of insurance may be a disadvantage. A young family man may not be able to buy as much protection. If he pays more dollars per thousand, he cannot buy as many thousands. A better choice for him would be: term insurance, or term insurance combined with straight life, or straight life insurance.

Endowment Policies—the face value (plus dividends in a mutual company) is paid to the insured person if he is living when the policy matures. He may receive the money in one cash payment, or in installments over a period of time. If he dies while receiving installment payments, any amount remaining will be paid to his estate.

Premiums are paid a certain number of years or to a certain age. Endowment policies cost more than other types of life insurance. Rates are higher during the time you pay. If the insured person dies before the policy matures, the beneficiary receives the face value of the policy.[2]

The same amount of premium will buy a larger amount of ordinary life insurance, thus more protection. At age 22, the premium for $1,000 on a 20-year endowment policy is about $47 a year, an ordinary life policy is about $15 a year.

If the insured person dies, either policy would pay the beneficiary $1,000. Therefore, it may not be wise for the family that needs income protection to buy an endowment policy.

The following chart indicates the average premium rates per $1,000 for each of these four types of policies.[3]

---

[2]Some endowment policies have an increasing death benefit to compensate for higher premiums paid should death occur during the premium paying period.

[3]*Ibid.*, p. 6.

TYPES OF LIFE INSURANCE POLICIES

Approximate premium rates per $1,000 of each of four types
of life insurance policies*

Bought at age	Term 5-year renewable & convertible	Straight Life	Limited Payment Life (Paid up at age 65)	Endowment 20-year
18	$ 8.65	$ 15.80	$ 16.90	$ 48.85
20	8.75	16.50	17.70	48.90
25	8.90	18.45	20.15	49.05
30	9.25	21.00	23.60	49.40
40	12.20	28.50	34.75	51.40
50	20.10	45.65	60.15	56.55

*Rates shown are approximate premium rates for life insurance protection for men.
Rates for women are somewhat lower.

(Rates of participating policies would be slightly higher, but the cost would be
lowered by annual dividends. Nonparticipating policy rates would be somewhat
lower than those shown and no dividends would be paid. Source: Institute of Life
Insurance, 1964.)

Variations or combinations of these four basic types of life insurance might include some of the following:

Mortgage Insurance

Home owners with substantial mortgages outstanding on their
property are often interested in some type of decreasing term insurance, referred to as mortgage insurance or home protection plan
insurance. The policy amount on straight term insurance remains the
same throughout the life of the policy. But with mortgage insurance,
the policy amount decreases over the years even though the annual
premium remains the same. Naturally, the premium will be less per
dollar of initial coverage, but as the amount decreases over the en-
suing years, the premium cost per dollar increases. In the last years
of such a policy, if it is continued, the cost per dollar coverage is
quite high.

The obvious purpose of this kind of insurance is to provide the
amount necessary to pay off the remaining balance of your home
mortgage if you should die before the mortgage is paid in full. Thus

the policy amount will decrease at the same approximate rate as the mortgage principal balance.

One plan works like this:

Year	Amount of insurance in 25-year plan
1	$ 25,000
5	23,075
10	19,900
15	15,600
20	9,775
25	1,875

If a home owner begins the policy at age 35, it would cost approximately $80 a year in premiums. Should he then die at age 45, the policy would pay $19,900 to his beneficiary, who could use the money to pay off the remaining mortgage balance. It should be understood that this is not required, but since the policy is intended for that purpose, it would likely be so used.

Family Income Plan Insurance

The family income policy combines term insurance with ordinary or straight life insurance. The term insurance portion of this type of policy pays the beneficiary a certain amount of cash each month from the date of the insured's death to the end of the policy term. A family-income-to-age-55 policy will pay monthly amounts to the beneficiary until the insured attains age 55. If the insured lives beyond age 55, the term insurance pays no benefits. However, the ordinary life portion of the policy will pay benefits regardless of the insured's age at death.

This type of policy is especially desirable for young families in need of income protection in addition to the usual requirements for life insurance. The policy's income provision is generally limited to the years when children are young and education expenses are demanding. A family income policy can help to support your family, educate your children, and pay your taxes and bills for you if you don't live to do these things yourself.

One insurance company offers four different plans: a 15- or 20-year family income plan, or a family-income-to-age-55 or age 65 plan. The former policies will pay your beneficiary monthly income for the remainder of the 15- or 20-year term after your death; the latter will pay until you become 55 or 65 years old, as previously explained. No payment is made if you live beyond these limits, except the lump sum.

Under a typical plan, if you die during the family income period, your family would receive the following benefits for $10,000 face amount of insurance:

Cash at death	$ 1,500
Income until the end of the income period .	$ 200 per month
Cash at the end of the income period	$10,000

Obviously, the benefits and costs for such policies will vary from one company to another, but this is representative. A 20-year family income policy issued at age 35 may cost you about $300 annually for a $10,000 policy as described above.[4]

Insurance Terminology

Some of the more common words used in discussing life insurance are defined as follows:

Automatic premium loan option—If your cash value is sufficient, your premiums will automatically be paid for you if you have not done so yourself by the end of the grace period. This becomes a loan to you against your policy.

Beneficiary—The person you name in your policy to receive the proceeds when you die.

---

[4]Some family income policies pay the face amount of the policy upon death and then continue monthly income or use the face amount to increase monthly income for the agreed-upon income period.

Cash or loan value—The amount of money you can receive if you should cancel your policy or if you wish to borrow against your policy while continuing with the same protection. If you borrow, you pay interest to the insurance company on such a loan. If you die before the loan is paid back, the policy proceeds will be reduced by the outstanding balance of the loan.

Conversion privileges—The right to change from one type of policy to another, usually without a medical re-examination, but at the rate then applicable for the new coverage. Such conversions are usually made from term into straight life or other insurance when the original purposes for the term policy are ended and the insured is better able to afford the increased premium costs of ordinary or endowment policies.

Disability waiver—Insurance premiums are paid for you by your insurance company if you are totally disabled for longer than a specified minimum time. Your protection continues at the same rate and no assessments for back premiums are made should your disability cease.

Dividends—That portion of a "participating" policyholder's premium payment which is not needed for present and future benefit payments, for contingencies, or for company operating expenses. Dividends may vary from year to year. When available (usually after two or three years' premiums are paid) they may be used either to reduce premiums, purchase paid-up insurance, or accumulate and add to the cash value or cash payment of the policy. They may, of course, also be withdrawn upon request.

Double indemnity clause—Twice the amount of the face value of the policy will be paid to the beneficiary if the insured dies accidentally.

Face value—The amount of insurance coverage listed on your policy.

Grace period—The number of days you have between the date the premium is due and the date when the policy can be cancelled because of nonpayment of premium.

Maturity—The time when the policy becomes payable as indicated in your policy, either at your death or when you reach a certain age, or after a certain length of time.

Nonparticipating policy—The policyholder does not participate in any of the profits of the company. The premium rates are fixed. There are no dividends to policyholders. Stock insurance companies usually issue such policies, with the stockholders rather than policyholders sharing in the profits of the company. (See also Participating policy.)

Paid-up insurance—The amount of insurance protection available for a stated length of time. No more premiums are due. If you should stop paying premiums on your present policy, your paid-up insurance would be the amount of coverage you could continue to have without additional payments. If this happens, the paid-up policy will, of course, be much less than the original amount. It may be either an ordinary paid-up policy, a paid-up endowment policy for a reduced amount, or perhaps term insurance for a decreasing amount for a specific length of time. Many policies do become paid-up at age 65 or after 20 years, or within other stated lengths of time.

Participating policy—Policyholders participate in the profits of the company. These are usually mutual insurance companies. Premium rates are fixed at an amount somewhat greater than the company expects will be needed under normal conditions to meet the costs of providing insurance. Policyholders then receive a refund, called a dividend, which represents that portion of the premium not needed for present or future costs by the company.

Policy—The legal contract between you and the insurance company which you receive upon entering into an agreement for insurance coverage.

Premium—The regular amount you pay for your policy at stated intervals of time. This is the cost of insurance.

Settlement options—The different ways in which the insurance company may pay money due at the maturity of the policy—regular installments for a fixed number of years or for the life of the beneficiary, one lump sum settlement, etc.

Other Life Insurance Protection

When you are totaling the amount of life insurance protection you have, don't fail to consider some of the following items.

Social Security—Not all clergymen are involved in the Social Security program, but if you are, there are certain benefits available for your survivors that you ought to be familiar with. For information on your specific benefits, check with your local Social Security Administration office.

The illustration below lists monthly payments available to your survivors depending upon your average earning level.

Examples of Monthly Payments Available to Those Covered by Social Security[5]

Average yearly earnings after 1950	$3,600	$4,800*	$6,600*
Widow 62 or over	$ 92.80	$ 112.20	$ 138.60
Widow at 60, no child	80.50	97.30	120.20
Widow under 62 and 1 child	168.60	204.00	252.00
Widow under 62 and 2 children ..	240.00	306.00	368.00
One surviving child	84.30	102.00	126.00
Two surviving children	168.60	204.00	252.00
Maximum family payment	240.00	309.20	368.00
Lump-sum death payment	255.00	255.00	255.00

*Because earnings of $4,800 and $6,600 cannot be credited for any year before 1959 and 1966 respectively, benefits in the last two columns will not generally be payable for some years to come.

---

[5]*Social Security Amendments 1965, A Brief Explanation,* U.S. Department of Health, Education, and Welfare, Social Security Administration, OASI-1965-1, GPO: 1965, 0-784-861, 3rd edition, 8/1965.

Your denomination's death benefit plan will provide certain payments to your beneficiaries upon your death. The plan of one denomination provides the following benefits: $16,000 at age 25 and decreasing each year by $250 until age 70, when the amount is $1,000 regardless of the age at death. Inquire at your denomination's headquarters for specific information about coverage for yourself.

Workmen's compensation is not likely to involve clergymen in a parish, but you should investigate and be certain of your coverage, if any.

Veteran's insurance is valuable coverage that should be continued by clergymen who have served in the armed forces.

Your Life Insurance Program

The amount of life insurance which you should carry depends upon your family's needs and circumstances as determined through a very careful analysis of your situation. While a rule of thumb might suggest that four or five times your annual salary ought to be minimum coverage, this too will vary with individuals and their needs.

Foremost, though, you should concentrate your coverage on yourself, on the family wage earner, although some men will insist upon greater coverage on their wives on the assumption that the cost of providing care and assistance for a family without a mother is quite expensive. Nevertheless, the principal coverage should be on the wage earner's life. Where there are young children, term insurance, straight life, or a family income plan are good plans. Remember, again, that you can get more than twice the coverage from an ordinary life policy than from an endowment policy and even more coverage for the same dollars with term insurance.

Since older persons with fewer family responsibilities may be interested in retirement income or investments, they may want other types of coverage. Endowment policies, as previously explained, offer an opportunity to build up higher cash values but offer less protection for the same cost than other types of insurance.

Before deciding on changes in your insurance program, talk over your needs and your ability to pay with a qualified insurance agent or your banker. Because life insurance is a very specialized field, most people quickly get lost and confused in the maze of insurance terminology and procedure and need expert help.

In selecting the person who will advise you on your insurance program, several considerations ought to be kept in mind. The insurance company which your agent represents ought to be financially sound and offer a wide variety of policies at prices that are competitive in order that you can select the type of coverage best for you. Your agent should be willing to offer you sound insurance advice whether or not he sells a policy to you. He should carry the C.L.U. (Chartered Life Underwriter) designation or at least be in the business full time. If he is your age or younger, his relationship with you can be expected to continue during the years when you will want and need his advice.

A Life Insurance Record

A valuable aid for you in evaluating your insurance coverage, as well as for others who may need to know your insurance program, is a record similar to that illustrated.

LIFE INSURANCE POLICIES RECORD

Policy number	Company	Agent	Insured	Beneficiary	Face amount	Type of coverage	Premium due dates	
							Amt.	Due date

LIFE INSURANCE PREMIUM PAYMENT RECORD

Payment Schedule	Policy No._____ Due Date_____ Amount_____		Policy No._____ Due Date_____ Amount_____		
Date	Paid	Cash value	Paid	Cash value	

Other Types of Insurance

Obviously there would be less need for insurance if we could accurately determine the time of death or when some other catastrophe or illness or accident or property damage would occur. Death is certain; other calamities are not, yet almost one out of every twelve families will suffer a calamity in any year. Thus, the possibility of your family's involvement in some calamity in the foreseeable future must be reckoned with.

If the time of these events were known, each of us would attempt to make adequate provision for funds to replace or pay for or otherwise protect ourselves against the loss to be incurred. In the absence of such certainties, however, it is important to protect ourselves and our families as best we can against those risks to which we are exposed. Insurance provides this protection.

When several persons contribute to the same fund at a predetermined rate based on the experiences of average costs for the particular catastrophe covered, such a group of people can be protected. It is unlikely that all families within the group will suffer the same calamity at the same time, but it is probable that some of the families will suffer that particular calamity within a given period of time. Those who do need help, therefore, have resources available to them in an amount far exceeding their premium contribution simply because many people have contributed to the fund. This is a fundamental principle of insurance coverage. Needless to say, the higher the incidence of occurrence as well as the higher the average cost of a covered calamity plus the fewer the persons covered, the greater will be the premium cost to each policyholder.

Health Insurance

Next to life insurance, various forms of health insurance are the most popular type of insurance coverage in America today. In 1963 nearly 80% of all Americans had hospitalization insurance, and coverage for other types of medical expenses, such as major medical, surgical, and disability, has increased rapidly.

Hospital insurance coverage under most plans pays for all charges incurred during a hospital stay, including room, board, operating room, X-rays, medicines, and so forth. Outpatient service (receiving treatment at a hospital without being a bed patient) is usually excluded from such coverage. Limits on the amount paid for room charges may be a dollar amount or that which is customarily charged for a semi-private room. But essentially, most hospitalization policies pay the entire cost of your hospital stay, or most of it, up to a maximum number of days. Your policy will describe the details of your plan for you.

Surgical insurance is coverage for doctors' fees. Your policy will list a schedule of fees which are paid for certain types of surgical procedures and other services performed by your doctor for you. This coverage is seldom the full amount which your doctor will charge, but substantial coverage can be obtained through most surgical policies.

Major medical or catastrophe insurance is just that. Payment is made for the big hospital and surgical bills. Since many hospital policies limit their payments to a maximum number of days in the hospital for any one illness, and surgical policies usually have a top limit of $350 to $500 for any one surgical procedure, major medical insurance is valuable for payment of expenses for long and expensive illnesses which are not covered by the standard hospital-surgical policies.

A typical policy will pay 80% of all expenses not covered by a standard hospital-surgical plan, after the insured has paid the deductible amount, often about $100. Or if no base plan is carried, $200 or $500 or some other agreed-on amount of hospital expenses must be paid first by the insured. The insurance company then pays 80% of the rest up to an agreed-on maximum for each illness, often up to $10,000. The details, of course, will be written into your policy. The cost of such a policy will depend upon the risks incurred by the insurance company. The greater the deductible amount, the less expensive the policy.

Disability insurance provides for a regular weekly income in the event you are unable to perform the regular duties of your work due to an illness or accident. Your policy will pay you whatever weekly amount you have agreed upon and have paid premiums for. The greater the amount you desire, of course, the greater the cost of such a policy to you.

Clergymen's families ought to carry some type of health insurance, especially if there are children. It is interesting to note, however, that recent statistics indicate that income is a more important factor than age or children or occupation in determining health insurance coverage.[6] Many denominations consider such coverage important and thus provide coverage for the individual pastor with an inexpensive group policy made available for the minister's family. The denomination pays the premium for the man; he pays for the family. The rising cost of medical care makes such coverage extremely important for the family with limited means and growing children.

Major medical coverage is also desirable, usually very inexpensive, and becoming more and more important and popular. It is a particularly valuable coverage for long illnesses or expensive operations to which older persons are most susceptible. However, younger

---

[6] *Health Insurance Coverage,* U.S. National Center for Health Statistics, July 1962-June 1963 (Vital and Health Statistics Series 10, No. 11), August 1964.

families, with limited resources, may also suffer costly accidents or illnesses, to which a major medical policy would make significant contributions.

Disability insurance becomes important if the wage earner is disabled for a long time. Most congregations will continue to pay their pastor in the event he is stricken and unable to work, at least for a reasonable time. But there can be a limit to this kind of generosity too. Disability insurance takes the burden off both the congregation and the minister. Clergymen enrolled in Social Security have disability coverage equal to their "retirement at age 65 benefits." See the complete Social Security benefits scheduled on page 116.

Your family's coverage must be determined by your needs, your desires, your circumstances, and your ability to pay the necessary premiums. Costs will vary from one policy to another and from one company to another. Check the benefits promised carefully. Compare with similar policies. The least expensive policy is not always the best. Be sure you are getting the type of coverage you need and want.

Medicare for Clergymen

The 1965 amendments to the Social Security Act contain significant provisions affecting ministers and their families. Prior to the effective date of the new health insurance program on July 1, 1966, Dr. Robert J. Myers, chief actuary of the Social Security Administration and chairman of the Benefits Committee of the Board of Pensions of the Lutheran Church in America, prepared a detailed statement of those provisions most significant for ministers. Portions of that statement follow.

The Medicare program "consists of two parts, hospital insurance and supplementary medical insurance. The former is concerned primarily with hospital benefits and is available to Social Security beneficiaries and also to all other persons who are now age 65 or over (or will attain that age before 1968). The supplementary program is concerned primarily with physician services and is available on an individual elective basis to all persons regardless of Social Security status.

"The hospital insurance system provides a specific program of hospitalization and related benefits for all persons who are (1) aged 65 and over and (2) 'entitled' to monthly Social Security benefits. The term 'entitled' means that the individual meets all the statutory provisions governing eligibility for monthly benefits (old age, dependent, or survivor) and has filed an application therefor (which may be concurrent with application for hospitalization benefits). The term thus includes not only beneficiaries in current-payment status, but also those who are not drawing monthly benefits because they are continuing in substantial employment.

"The following benefits are provided:

"1. 90 days of semiprivate hospital care within a 'benefit period,' with a flat deductible of $40 during 1966-68 and possibly more later (if hospitalization costs rise). There is also a coinsurance payment of $10 (initially) for each hospital day beyond the 60th day. In addition, there is a deductible equal to the cost of the first three pints of blood used in a spell of illness. The hospital services covered include room and board, operating room, laboratory tests and X-rays, drugs, dressings, general nursing services, and services of interns and residents in training (but no other physician services, even though the doctor is on the hospital staff, or his services are arranged for and billed through the hospital).

"2. 100 days of post-hospital extended care within a 'benefit period,' when such services are furnished following transfer from a hospital (after at least three days of hospitalization) and are necessary for continued treatment of a condition for which the individual was hospitalized. Such care would be furnished in an 'extended care facility,' which is an institution that has in effect a transfer agreement with a hospital (or is under common control with a hospital) and that is, in essence, a skilled nursing facility (as defined in detail in the law). There is a coinsurance of $5 per day (initially) for each day beyond the 20th day. It should be noted that this benefit is not for custodial nursing home care, but rather for convalescent and re-cuperative care.

"3. 100 post-hospital home health service visits during the year following his most recent discharge from a hospital (after at least three days of hospitalization)—or from an extended care facility after such hospitalization. The plan for such services must be estab-lished within two weeks of such discharge. These services include visiting nurse services, therapy treatments, appliances, and medical supplies (other than drugs).

"4. 80 per cent of the cost of outpatient hospital diagnostic ser-vices in excess of a deductible equal to $20 (initially) with respect to services furnished during a 20-day period by a particular hospital.

"The 'benefit period' begins with the first day that an individual receives hospitalization benefits. It ends with the 60th consecutive day thereafter during each of which he has not been a patient in a hospital or an extended care facility. The benefits would first be available in July, 1966, except for post-hospital extended care benefits, which would first be available in January, 1967."[7]

For self-employed persons, these hospital and related benefits for Social Security beneficiaries are financed through the self-employ-ment tax which includes a specific provision for health insurance premiums, as noted in the self-employment tax rate schedule on page 118.

"The hospital benefit protection is also provided to any person aged 65 and over on July 1, 1966, who is not eligible as a Social Se-curity beneficiary, with certain minor exceptions. Persons who at-tain age 65 before 1968 also qualify for the hospital benefits, while those attaining age 65 after 1967 must have some Social Security coverage to qualify—namely, three quarters of coverage (which can be acquired at any time after 1936) for each year elapsing after 1965 and before the year of attainment of age 65. This transitional pro-

[7]Courtesy of the Commission on Press, Radio, and Television of the Lutheran Church in America, 231 Madison Ave., New York.

vision 'washes out' for men attaining age 65 in 1974 and for women attaining age 65 in 1972, since the fully-insured-status requirement for monthly benefits for such categories is then no greater than the special-insured status requirement. . . .

"The supplementary medical insurance system is to operate on a purely voluntary, individual-election basis, available to any individual aged 65 or over who chooses to participate, with certain minor exceptions.

"After a $50 calendar-year deductible, 80 per cent of covered medical expenses are reimbursed. There is a carry-over provision for expenses that went toward meeting the deductible in the last three months of the previous year. Also, any amount paid as an outpatient diagnostic deductible under hospital insurance counts as an incurred expense under the supplementary medical insurance plan. When necessary for diagnosis or treatment of a sickness or injury, the following medical services are covered:

"1. Physician and surgeon services (in home, office, and hospital), except for routine physical or eye examinations, etc.

"2. Outpatient psychiatric services—with 50 per cent coinsurance and maximum annual reimbursement of $250.

"3. Home health service visits (regardless of hospitalization)— maximum of 100 visits per year.

"4. Other medical services—diagnostic tests; X-ray and similar therapy; surgical dressings and splints; rental of iron lungs, oxygen tents, hospital beds, and similar equipment; prosthetic devices and artificial limbs and eyes; and ambulance service (under restricted conditions).

"Covered physicians' services are limited to those by a licensed doctor of medicine or osteopathy and to certain oral surgical procedures if performed by a doctor of dentistry or oral surgery.

"Benefits for physician services and other services that are not furnished by a 'provider of services' such as a hospital, extended care facility, or home health agency will be payable on the basis of 'reasonable charges.' Benefits for services furnished by such a provider will be payable on the basis of 'reasonable charges.'

"If the physician charges the patient on such basis, he may receive the 80 per cent payment directly from the program, but if he wishes to charge more, the patient will receive the 80 per cent payment on the basis of a receipted bill. Benefits will be available for services furnished after June, 1966.

"The covered individual will pay a premium that is set initially at a rate of $3 per month. . . . After 1967, the premium rate may be changed biennially by the Secretary of Health, Education, and Welfare to reflect the actual past experience and that anticipated in the future. The premium rate will be increased for those who do not enroll in the earliest period in which they could enroll—by 10 per cent for each full year of delay. Social Security beneficiaries will have the premiums automatically deducted from their benefit checks.

"The initial enrollment period extended to May 31, 1966. Persons attaining age 65 after 1965 can enroll in the seven-month period surrounding the month of their birthday.

"If an individual does not enroll at that time, he can do so only within the next three years and in a general enrollment period, which is October through December of each odd-numbered year beginning with 1967; with coverage effective beginning with the next July.

"An individual can elect to withdraw from the program during a general enrollment period or, if not paying premiums by the benefit-deduction method, by failure to pay the premium. After withdrawal, the individual can re-enroll (only once) if he does so within three years, in a general enrollment period."[8]

Many health insurance plans have been or will be radically modified by insurance companies for policyholders over age 65. Because Medicare is so comprehensive there is not much supplementary protection that can be provided for persons age 65 or over. The real need for a supplementary policy is for those families where only one

---

[8]*Ibid.*

member is over 65. Thus clergymen over 65 whose wives are under age 65, or vice versa, should consider such supplementary coverage.

Additional information on Medicare may be obtained from your local Social Security Administration office. Ask for the folder *A Brief Explanation of Medicare, Health Insurance for the Aged*.

Automobile Insurance

Automobile insurance coverage is varied, depending upon the company involved and the state in which you live. Obviously it is a very basic type of policy for clergymen. Of primary importance when you purchase or renew a policy is to know precisely what your policy says. Be sure you understand the basic provisions. Know for what kind of protection you are paying your premiums. Then, as soon as you receive your policy read it over carefully, even the fine print, to be certain that you know what is included. Some of the items which you may want to consider are the following.

Liability coverage includes bodily injury liability and property damage liability. Your policy sets a limit on the amount the company will pay for damages for which you are legally responsible because of bodily injury sustained by other persons or property damage caused by your automobile. This is often referred to by numbers such as 20-40-10 coverage, that is, up to $20,000 coverage for each person in an accident but not more than $40,000 coverage for bodily injury for each accident no matter how many people are involved. The $10,000 would be a limit on the property damage coverage available for any one accident. If you were sued as the result of an accident, these are the maximum amounts the insurance company would pay on your behalf. Any liability above that becomes your personal responsibility.

Medical payments, not liabilities, but medical expenses incurred by others and for which you are legally responsible, are also listed in your policy, $2,000 to $5,000 being a common amount. Your insurance company will pay up to that amount for reasonable medical expenses incurred by others for which you are liable. A major medical feature may also be included here which will pay for expenses incurred by others over and above coverage provided in the medical payments section.

Comprehensive coverage obligates the insurance company to pay for any loss to your automobile, except losses caused by collision. You will be paid the actual cost of repair or replacement if your car is stolen or damaged by fire, larceny, earthquake, windstorm, hail, water, flood, and so forth. Your policy lists the specific items included.

Deductible collision insurance, usually written for $50 or $100 deductible, means that you will agree to pay the stated deductible amount and the insurance company will pay the rest of any cost you incur for repair of your automobile due to an accident or other cause regardless of whether you are at fault or not. Obviously, if the other person is at fault, his insurance company, if he has one, will pay the costs.

Emergency road service is another familiar coverage feature that pays you for expenses incurred for hauling or transporting or otherwise assisting you, should you need emergency service to make your car function properly. Such coverage of course does not include the cost of repairs unless caused by accident or one of the other items specifically listed in your policy.

Total disability coverage provides for a stated weekly payment to you in the event you are totally disabled in an accident. Death indemnity for an amount stated in your policy is also available. "Uninsured motorist" coverage is receiving increasingly wider acceptance. Of course, many other provisions which you may want to consider in your automobile insurance coverage are available through your agent.

Most important, though, you should read your policy very carefully to be certain that you are adequately covered in the way that you think you are. It is particularly desirable for clergymen to be adequately insured when operating their cars. Not that they are less careful than other drivers, but because they do so much driving they are subject to the possibilities of accident more often. Furthermore, the number of friends and church members who are frequently transported by the pastor afford added chances for liability in case of an accident.

Property Insurance

You can buy insurance for almost any purpose, as has been stated before, and more and more types of insurance are becoming available and desirable. Recently many home owners have discovered that they can get adequate coverage for a variety of purposes all in one insurance policy. While it is not uncommon to have policies for each type of coverage desired, most families now have a "home owner's policy" which in one policy provides the varieties of protection most families desire. Despite its title, this type of policy is available to clergymen even though they may not own their own homes. All other provisions except those specifically applicable to dwellings owned by the policyholder would be desirable for the clergyman in a church-owned parsonage.

The most frequent provisions of such policies include the following items:

1. Dwellings are protected under fire and extended coverage provisions. This is the most important feature for the home owner. This includes coverage in case of fire, of course, but it may also include these perils: windstorm, hail, explosion, riot, civil commotion, aircraft and vehicle damage, and damage by smoke. Additional coverage at additional cost may include damage from water (but not from floods), from steam and hot water heating systems, from vandalism and malicious mischief, from trees and other falling objects, and many other hazards. Your policy will spell out for you in much detail all the perils covered.

2. Scheduled or unscheduled personal property may be covered against similar types of perils. This is coverage for damage to your furniture and appliances, clothes, and personal belongings. Perhaps the most important additional coverage in this category is theft insurance, not only theft from your home but theft at any time or place of any of your personal belongings. Again your policy will be very specific about all the details. Maximum benefits available under either of the above provisions are written into your policy.

3. Many fire insurance policies carry a coinsurance clause, thus reducing the premium costs and in effect making the insured a coinsurer with the insurance company. The typical policy will list an 80% coinsurance clause. Your agent will explain this provision in detail for you.

The reasoning behind such coverage is this: Even if your home burns to the ground, its full value is not destroyed since the foundation walls at least are left, together with any concrete slab floors. To insure the house for its total value therefore is not necessary. Under a coinsurance clause, the company will normally pay 80% of the value of your home if there is a complete loss.

However, it is important that the amount of insurance you carry be equal to at least 80% of the value of your home. If it is less, then any loss you incur, partial or total, will not be fully paid by the insurance company.

For instance, if you carry $20,000 on your house under a coinsurance provision, then suffer a $5,000 loss and a subsequent appraisal reveals your house is worth $30,000, you are under-insured (insurance required is 80% of $30,000, or $24,000), and you cannot collect the full damages. The following formula calculates your actual coverage:

$$\frac{\text{Amount of insurance carried (\$20,000)}}{\text{Amount of insurance required (\$24,000)}} \times \text{Loss (\$5,000)}$$

equals the Amount paid ($4,167)

On the other hand, if you had carried $24,000 of insurance, the $5,000 loss would have been paid in full.

In addition to this type of coverage on your dwelling, your personal property coverage may also be carried in the same way. For that kind of coverage though a careful inventory of your personal goods is extremely important, not only to arrive at the insurance coverage needed, but to be able to list what might be lost in a fire. An inventory schedule such as is shown in Chapter 2 will be extremely valuable in this connection.

4. Comprehensive personal liability insurance coverage, including bodily injury and property damage, is listed as a maximum amount for each occurrence, perhaps $25,000, as so much per person, say $10,000, and up to perhaps $5,000 for property damage. This protection is important when someone is injured by a fall on your icy sidewalk or a child is hit by your boy with a baseball bat. You are covered for any legal obligations incurred on account of bodily or property damage alleged by others to be your responsibility. This coverage extends beyond the premises of your home also. Again, read your policy carefully. It is very specific.

5. Medical payments coverage is available to pay, up to a specified amount for each person, perhaps $500, medical expenses incurred by those who may sustain bodily injury caused by an accident while in your home or even away from your home if the injury results from your activity or that of your family or in your employment or because of the condition of your home.

6. Physical damage caused by you to the property of others is also a standard protection and may be limited to $250 for each occurrence. If your son hits a baseball through the neighbor's window, you are covered by this provision for the cost of replacing that window.

In many parts of the nation home owner's policies carry a deductible provision. It works the same way as the deductible on your automobile insurance. You pay the first $50 or $100, or whatever the deductible amount is, for damage you cause, while the insurance company pays the rest. Obviously, this means that your rate will be less because claims against the company will be less. Some states require this provision, some don't. You will need to inquire about the provisions in the state where you live.

Of course, there are many other types of insurance available: boat owner's coverage, farm liability, business insurance, and others. When you review your insurance coverage with your agent, he will gladly tell you what is available and advise you on your needs. Trust your agent. He will help you to secure the best and the least expensive coverage, and he will help settle your claims whenever a loss is suffered.

Insurance is not cheap, but it is important protection for those who have something valuable to protect. Ministers and their families have many needs and quite often considerable possessions and thus are subject to losses just as anyone else is. You should seriously consider adequate insurance coverage as a very important part of your family's spending plan.

Chapter 5

Buying a House

Fifty years ago it would have been difficult to find a church that did not provide a parsonage along with its other emoluments and fringe benefits for its pastor. In fact, the quality, age, size, and location of the parsonage may often have been a decisive factor in the acceptance of a call. In the history of the church, providing a parsonage has been an important part of church finances and ministerial family life. Even among other professions fifty years ago such procedures were not at all unusual. Many communities were built up around towns where a large company had provided its workers with homes, community centers, and a general store.

But times have changed. Industrial advances, economic growth, the rise of labor unions, and personal ambitions have forced company housing to be replaced by other more adequate remuneration. Consequently, salaries have been increased, working conditions bettered, fringe benefits enlarged to such an extent that the working man has now been able—and encouraged—to buy his own home. The tremendous increase in suburban housing developments vividly attests to this.

Churches, however, have lagged sadly behind in this transformation. Among the most educated professionals, ministers alone continue to be burdened with an archaic system of parsonages, manses, and rectories. This is not to say that all parsonages are archaic or inadequate. Indeed, many are quite modern and pretentious. But the system persists, though in few other professions is a home furnished as part of a man's compensation for his work.

74

It is acknowledged that many a clergyman would be hard pressed financially to provide a home for his family on short notice. Furthermore, many clergymen simply prefer the convenience of using a home owned by the church. It is obviously a much simpler matter. Moreover, many church-owned parsonages are spacious and modern, most convenient and usually elegantly furnished far beyond what a minister could possibly provide with his own investment. Many pastors are extremely satisfied with the present situation and would be most reluctant to change from their status as "renters" to home owners.

But there is a growing number of clergymen in all denominations who are clamoring for a change in the system. Those who have persuaded their church councils and vestries of the wisdom of a change are now receiving increased salaries with a "house allowance" included. These pastors no longer have a parsonage which may be entirely inadequate for their needs or extremely adverse to their tastes forced upon them. They are now able to make their own choices.

This is a healthy trend. It indicates movement toward an increased identification of the clergyman with the society to which he tries to minister, for home ownership includes involvement in such mundane matters as building materials and legal terminology familiar to many parishioners.

Indeed, there can be a considerable listing of "reasons why" in support of this growing concern for a clergyman's securing his own housing. A few of the more important considerations are mentioned here.

First of all, although not most important, home ownership requires participation in the local tax program, making the pastor's family a very definite supporting part of the community. Because of this involvement and subsequent better understanding of their neighbors' related problems, the pastor and his family may well become more substantial contributors to the welfare of the community in which they live. They may very well speak out on those issues for which their tax dollars are being used. The issue becomes much more personal when the minister's own dollars are being used to support schools, police, fire departments, libraries, and the other community services. He will vote for their intelligent use, and he will become as concerned a member of the community as any one of his neighbors.

Another reason may be this: home ownership provides a keen sense of accomplishment, of permanency, of attachment, of security. It is to the credit of American clergymen and their families that they have usually been quite secure and at home wherever they are and under whatever circumstances they may be living. And yet, home ownership, unlike parsonage living, provides a sense of "living in my own home." "This belongs to me, and I can do with it whatever I want without consulting a parsonage committee!" Along with this sense of freedom, of course, goes responsibility. The home owner cannot call some church committee to look after leaky plumbing in the middle of the night. Now he has to fix it himself!

A familiar argument for home ownership by clergymen is the idea of building up an equity. Substantial savings or equity can be built up over a period of time and amount to a significant sum. On the basis of today's "longest term, lowest payment" policy, however, it takes quite a while to build up an equity except through larger down payments. But then few home owners expect to pay for their homes in full—ever—at least not *this* house, for they will some day move on to a larger one. Yet, over a period of time and coupled with increases in property values, equity actually can be built up which will certainly eventually accrue to the minister's benefit.

A fourth reason: Home ownership may very well be an inducement to a longer tenure in one place. It's rather simple to pack up and move out of the church's parsonage, but selling your own home and taking care of the details involved may prove to be a real burden. On the other hand, precisely because of the permanency involved in home buying, if the relationship between pastor and people deteriorates after a time, a church may not be able to encourage a pastor to move on as graciously as otherwise. So it works both ways!

Surely the pastor who knows about mortgages, insurance, taxes, escrow accounts, closing costs, interest, and the general problems of house maintenance will be far more familiar with some of the most prevalent and basic problems affecting families today. Obviously, home ownership will provide some valuable experience in this area of counseling. Few "parsonage" clergymen can sit down with their parishioners and, when the situation demands it, intelligently discuss such financial matters with them. They are simply lacking in the necessary experience. There may very well be a significant psychological effect upon a membership of home owners when they know that their pastor is familiar with some of their own home ownership problems.

We must also recognize, however, that there are several distinct disadvantages to eliminating the parsonage. In those denominations where pastors move or are moved frequently, this would produce considerable hardship and inconvenience. Selecting, buying, and selling a home is not the sort of thing one does every three or four years. Doing these things at all takes considerable time and usually means an extra move for the new pastor and his family from the rented place they first moved into to the home they finally select.

Furthermore, not every congregation is located in the kind of neighborhood where a pastor may want to buy a home or where such an investment is good or even possible. It is very important for the church to serve the downtown communities of our large cities, but it is not always possible to buy decent living quarters for a pastor's family in such areas. Congregations in the midst of modern apartment complexes pose similar disadvantages to the purchase of a home.

And then sometimes, perhaps quite often, a home is sold for a loss, or at least for less than was paid for it. The clergyman must accept this possibility. And yet when the figures are finally totaled, the facts may reveal that no more was lost than would have been spent had the man been paying rent instead. In the meantime, though, there has certainly been the satisfaction of enjoying one's own home and doing with it what one likes.

Unfortunately though, for some pastors, many congregations continue to harbor the notion that the church-owned parsonage is desirable. Certainly this system offers a good deal of stability to the parsonage situation for both the church and the pastor. Conscientious congregations who still insist on providing the familiar parsonage should, then, build adequate and spacious homes that are truly designed for the pastor and his family and their needs.

A church magazine[1] recently listed these unique needs for a parsonage:

1. A minister's study easily accessible to the front hall, or having an outside door so that parishioners may enter without interrupting the minister's family. There should be built-in bookcases and cabinets.

2. Five bedrooms.

3. Reception hall.

4. Family room in the basement, to be used by church groups also, with a fireplace if possible below the one in the living room on the first floor, and an adjoining kitchenette for serving coffee and dessert.

5. A lavatory in the basement.

6. A laundry in the basement with proper connections for appliances.

7. Small full bath on the first floor; a large bathroom on the second floor for children.

8. A garage in back of the house with a large double driveway for off-street parking for church groups.

---

[1]Philip M. Larson Sr. and Philip M. Larson Jr., "The Parsonage—Asset or Liability?" *Church Management*, XXXIX (October, 1962), p. 14.

9. Back door going directly to the basement room so that parishioners can go directly to the place of meeting.

Obviously the list can be changed in any desirable way.

While a rental allowance is the obvious alternative to the church-owned parsonage, allowing the minister to rent or purchase a home as he pleases, a new idea has been suggested that may prove desirable for many pastors and congregations.

This idea involves a plan whereby the church provides the payments for the house which the minister owns. A typical plan may include an agreement between the church and the pastor whereby an annual allowance of $2,400 is provided from the church budget for the payment of principal, interest, and insurance on the pastor's home. The pastor's salary is arranged as though a parsonage were provided. An additional allowance for utilities is also stipulated in the church budget. The minister in turn provides the funds for a down payment, perhaps $1,000, either from his own savings, or by a loan from the church, or from some other source.

The church then actually purchases a home of the minister's choice and makes all the payments required on the indebtedness according to the allowance previously agreed upon in its budget. Because the church may be able to secure a lower rate of interest on a loan and is likely not required to pay property taxes, there can be a substantial saving under this plan for a minister and his congregation.

When the minister leaves the congregation, the home is given to him and title is transferred to his name. He can then do with it what he likes—sell, rent, whatever he chooses. In the meantime, though, he has been able to consider it his own home and in fact may very well have put additional funds of his own into the home's upkeep and improvement.

Some pastors see this as a good opportunity in the future. At least, it ought to be given consideration by the clergyman faced with the choice of a church-owned parsonage or a home of his own.

When You Buy That Dream House

If you have finally decided that buying a home is the thing you want to do and can do and your church has agreed to provide the necessary house allowance for you, then a whole list of new decisions face you and your family. And all of these matters must be considered carefully. Many of your decisions must now be made on the advice of a competent attorney or architect or banker or some other expert in a field where you as a clergyman are likely to know very little.

First consideration must be the cost and size of house you have in mind, and the one will very nearly determine the other. As was mentioned previously, a good rule of thumb is that the cost of your home should not exceed two and a half times your annual income. Or, put another way, your monthly mortgage payments should not exceed one-fourth of your monthly take-home pay. This will set the maximum on the amount you should consider in purchasing a home.

Then consider the space requirements for your family's needs today and for several years to come, or the space you think you would like to have. Then, if you expect to build your own home or buy a relatively new one, you can add up the possible costs quite quickly. A quick estimate, variable, of course, depending upon what you include in your home, can be totaled if you know the average cost per square foot for building in your community. Ask a reputable builder for an estimate. Perhaps it will be twelve or fifteen dollars per square foot. If so, compute the total square footage of living space you will need, multiply by the estimated cost, and you have a rough idea of what your house may cost. If the figure is beyond your purchase ability but you need the space, consider buying an older house, one that is roomy and in good condition. Look around your town, and you may find a bargain. Don't forget, though, that it may cost a significant amount to repair and that annual maintenance costs may be large, too. While a new home is virtually maintenance free for many years, it does cost more for its size to begin with than an older home will.

So, whether you buy a new home, build your own on your own lot, or get an old one will depend largely on your tastes, your needs, and the costs involved. You will do well to consider carefully all aspects of each situation. Know what you face before you jump off the deep end. Be prepared to face the costs—expect the unexpected —of whatever decisions you make. Houses don't usually come very inexpensively, though you can still find a bargain by careful and patient shopping. But no house or lot will be perfect. Make your decisions, and then enjoy the freedom of being one of the millions of Americans owning their own homes.

But before you launch out on one of the most expensive projects you will probably ever encounter, there are a few other items which you need to consider rather carefully. You will want to investigate the location of your new home—its neighborhood, shopping centers, schools, buses, and so forth. How close is it to your church and to other churches of the same denomination? Consider the approximate value of the other homes in the area. Don't buy or build a house that is obviously more expensive than the others nearby. Should you want to sell sometime, the proximity of lower priced housing will tend to reduce the value of your house. A less expensive house in a more expensive neighborhood is better for resale possibilities.

Few young families today expect to live in the house they are buying now for the rest of their lives. As the children grow up, or companies transfer employees, or for any number of reasons—changing neighborhoods, encroachment of industry, freeway construction, etc.—families will sell their homes, move elsewhere, and buy again. Each move will probably be to a higher priced house, and the cycle of home buying will start all over again. Good or bad, this is the trend in modern America. And clergymen, rather than being an exception to the trend, will probably move even more frequently than most people because of the nature of their occupation.

So, consider costs and size, neighborhoods, conveniences, schools, proximity of business districts, busy streets, etc., carefully. Don't rush in. Chances are there's another house at the same price not too far away. Barter for a fair price on what you want. Then get what you want at a price you can afford to pay.

Once you have decided on a particular lot and house, have your banker appraise the property for you. Then if you are agreed on a purchase price with the seller, you will want to "sew up" the deal as soon as possible with a formal contract of sale. That is, you can assure the seller that you want the place by signing a contract to that effect and making a small down payment toward the purchase price. This will bind the seller to sell to you, and you agree to buy at the stipulated price, or else forfeit your "earnest money" payment. You will probably agree in writing to close the deal within thirty days since it usually takes about that much time to get all the necessary papers in order. If you are arranging for a loan, there is a considerable amount of work needed to complete such arrangements. At any rate, a contract of sale is essential for the protection of both parties to the sale and gives your attorney opportunity to prepare the necessary documents unhurriedly.

Once again, your attorney will be able to prepare all the papers you will need, and he will carefully check over the papers prepared for you by the seller's attorney. Your initial contract, though, among other things, should include full names of both parties, terms of the sale and purchase, legal description of the property involved, any special arrangements regarding furnishings, draperies, carpets, etc., guarantee of good title or furnishing of a title policy, return of down payment if financing is not available or for any other stipulated reason, agreement on payment of closing costs, as well as anything else you think important and necessary for your protection until you get a deed and title to the land.

You will probably need to finance this project because you won't have all the necessary cash available to pay for it. Mortgage loans are usually available in three ways—G.I., F.H.A., and conventional. Following World War II, Congress enacted legislation which afforded discharged servicemen the opportunity to purchase homes and borrow practically the entire purchase price of their new homes at a lower than usual interest rate. This was made possible by certain government guarantees of funds. Several restrictions were placed on the making of such loans, but whenever possible, servicemen used them to considerable advantage.

Federal Housing Administration insured loans continue to be a popular source of mortgage money, although housing requirements and loan regulations are much more stringent than for conventional loans. Contrary to popular ideas, an F.H.A. loan is not money borrowed from the Government. Your lending institution is lending the money, the same as for a conventional loan. But the F.H.A. has insured your mortgage against your failure to pay it in full. This insurance protects the lending institution against loss on your loan. It does not insure you in any way. Nevertheless, there are benefits to be derived for the borrower on such loans as described in the Federal Housing Administration's booklet *FHA Home Owner's Guide* #100, revised July, 1962.

1. The lender is able to make the loan on more liberal terms than it otherwise could.

2. The F.H.A. limits the interest rate and the other charges that can be made.

3. The F.H.A. appraises the home to make sure that it is adequate security for the loan. The builder or seller is required to give the buyer a written statement of the amount at which the F.H.A. values the property.

4. If application for mortgage insurance is made before construction of the house begins, the F.H.A. reviews the plans and specifications to see that they meet F.H.A. minimum property standards, and makes inspections during construction.

5. The F.H.A. determines that the transaction into which the buyer is entering appears to be a sound one.

And that is all the F.H.A. does for you. You still build or buy your own home. The F.H.A. will see that its interests are protected and in so doing will be protecting your interests too. But the owner is still responsible and must ultimately be satisfied that the house is good.

Naturally, such insurance is not free. In fact, you will pay one-half of one percent on the outstanding balance of your loan for your F.H.A. mortgage insurance premium. From such premiums administrative expenses of the F.H.A. are paid so that your taxes are not involved in the support of this agency.

With respect to prepayments on your F.H.A. loan, if you should come into a windfall, you may pay up to 15% of the original mortgage amount above your regular monthly payments in any one year. If you want to pay more than that or want to pay off the loan, then a prepayment penalty of 1% of the original amount of the loan will be required. This you agree to do with any F.H.A. loan.

A few other items: Under F.H.A. issued loans you will still take care of paying your own taxes, assessments, and insurance. It is up to you to provide the necessary maintenance and to keep your house in good repair.

Conventional mortgage loans, on the other hand, are made by a lending institution to you without any other agency's assurance or guarantee. The mortgage arrangements and terms are worked out between you and the lending institution. The house you buy or build is not inspected by a Federal Government agency officer, although it will be inspected periodically by the proper municipality officers in accord with your local building code. While the lending institution will be very much concerned with the quality of the work on your house, you must be your own inspector, or your architect will be, over the progress on your home.

Conventional loans usually require a larger down payment on the total cost than an F.H.A. or G.I. loan, primarily because of the lender's greater risk. Effective interest rates, however, are comparable with other types of loans. Terms of repayment will be arranged as agreed by you and the lender. Conventional loans often involve less "red tape," are easier to secure in most circumstances, and generally

provide a very convenient way in which to borrow money. Details
on the arrangements best for you will vary according to the requirements of your lending institution and the kind of mortgage terms
you request. Ask your banker for full information.

Interest rates may vary from 5% to 7% depending on the availability of money and the risks involved for the lender. It may be
worth your while to shop around for the lowest interest rate you
can get; but then be certain the other terms of the loan will be favorable also, such as closing costs and prepayment penalty clauses. These
can be significant added costs that will more than offset an otherwise
favorable loan with lower interest rates. When you have completed
your loan and begin making payments, the lender will take the interest you owe out of each monthly payment first and apply the
remainder of your payment to reducing the amount of your loan.

Usually interest is calculated each month on the amount of money
you still owe. Therefore, each payment you make will include a
smaller share for interest and a larger amount for principal. You may
want to reduce your loan as quickly as possible in order to avoid
high interest costs. If you have a $30,000 loan, you will pay more
than $61,000 on principal and interest if you extend the loan over
a thirty-year period at 5½% interest! Of course, you have an equity
of at least $30,000, and presumably more at the end of that time, if
there are no adverse effects against the market value of your home.
And if you had paid the same amount in rent all those years, you
would have nothing whatever to show for it at the end of thirty
years.

Other Matters Related to Buying a Home

Escrow accounts are often established by lending institutions to
provide funds for the payment of insurance and taxes for you. If such
an arrangement is worked out, your monthly payment will include
interest and principal on your loan as well as one-twelfth of the estimated insurance costs and taxes for the year. Escrow accounts are

computed in such a way that whenever your insurance and taxes come due, usually once a year, there will be enough money accumulated in this fund to pay these costs. In a sense your escrow account is a savings plan whereby you pay monthly those costs that are due and payable annually.

Fire and extended coverage insurance on your home will be required by the lender in an amount at least equal to your loan. For your own protection you ought to consider having additional coverage. About 80% of the value of your home (not including the land) is sufficient, depending again on the kind of house you have. A reputable insurance agent can give you good advice, as explained in the previous chapter.

Young families with large mortgages will do well to purchase what was described in Chapter 4 as a decreasing term insurance policy on the life of the husband. This type of life insurance may cost $5 to $8 a month depending on the amount of the mortgage. It is term insurance, which means there are no dividends or cash or loan value involved. It is decreasing insurance because the face amount of the policy, as explained in the chapter on insurance, decreases as the balance owed on your mortgage decreases. Its purpose is to protect the family by paying off the balance of your mortgage in the event of the husband's death. This is valuable but inexpensive insurance that clergymen ought to purchase if they are buying a home.

When you buy property you will also want to protect yourself against claims on the property due to a faulty title. Your attorney will make an examination of the deed records for you, a kind of history of the property over the past fifty years or so to be certain there are no claims for ownership against it and that you are actually buying the entire interest in the property. He will also examine the necessary records to be certain that there are no liens or judgments against the property and that the taxes are paid up. He may give you an abstract, a rather bulky book listing all the previous owners and other information about the property. Or you may simply receive a letter from him stating that he has examined the deed records and other documents at the county courthouse and finds no fault with the deed or any outstanding judgments or liens against the property. Or in some states you may get a title insurance policy. For a lump sum premium based on the current valuation of the property or amount of your mortgage, a title company will insure you against defects or claims by others to the title for your lot. In return for the premium paid, the title company guarantees to pay to the mortgage holder or the purchaser, if an additional premium is paid, the face amount of the policy should anyone ever make an enforceable claim of prior interest in the property against you.

In addition to the foregoing, there are several other matters related to house buying and selling which you should check into before making any commitments. Real estate agent's fees are involved in almost every home sale, but this is the responsibility of the seller. A contract is made between the person wanting to sell and an agent, with terms written out specifying a 5% to 6% commission due the agent if a buyer is located who agrees to meet the terms of sale set by the seller. Once such a buyer has been found by the agent, the seller is obligated to sell on the terms agreed upon or to pay the commission even if he changes his mind about selling. As stated above, the agent's fee is the seller's obligation; the buyer has no responsibility for it unless otherwise agreed in the contract of sale.

An agreement with a real estate agent, known as a "listing," may be an exclusive one, in which the seller agrees to give the agent exclusive rights to try to sell his home within a specified time—30 to 60 to 90 days. If no buyer is located in that time, the contract ends. However, the fine print in the contract should be read. If the house is sold shortly after the exclusive contract ends, the agent could claim that his efforts in part made the sale possible and that he should receive some fee. The contract will indicate the possibilities of this event. Or a seller may agree to let an agent list his home, but not on an exclusive basis. Then he may contract on the same basis with other agents. Whichever agent finds a buyer first gets the commission.

Closing costs are a part of every real estate transaction, and they can be quite expensive depending on the circumstances of the sale. If you are buying an unimproved lot and can pay cash for it, then attorney's fees and recording fees are about all that is involved. On the other hand, if you are purchasing a home, you may get involved with refinancing loan costs, setting up initial escrow account balances, apportioning taxes due, paying attorney's fees, using a title company (and paying for their services), getting title insurance, and a whole host of other items, all of which may involve considerable costs. Be sure of what you have to pay ahead of time. Indeed, secure an itemized list. A few inquiries will get you all the information you need, and you will be much better prepared for the closing experience than if you are caught off guard. Unless you and the other party agree differently, seller and buyer share in these costs and pay their respective portions.

If you are in doubt about the boundaries of your property, a survey should be made. A qualified surveyor will get a scale drawing of your lot prepared for you showing boundaries, dimensions, and the location of all improvements. Furthermore, the surveyor will bury steel rods at each corner of your lot so that you can always locate the corners if you need to.

An independent appraisal is very desirable whenever you are considering selling or buying real estate. It is simply a good idea to have an impersonal expert advise you about the current worth of the property you are considering. Appraisers are familiar with the market, with surrounding land values, with the area, the future potential, and many other items you don't know anything about. It may cost you some money, but you will know if the lot and house are worth the price you are bidding or asking.

If you are requesting a mortgage to purchase property, the lending institution will make its own appraisal for determining the maximum amount of your loan, usually about 70 to 75 per cent of the total value on conventional loans, but much higher on insured loans. Tax officials will have previously appraised the lot and house for tax purposes, and you can get this information from the proper books of record at the courthouse. But this may not be as reliable an estimate of value as an independent appraiser's current estimate of worth. Know what you are buying and get a good deal. Or know the value of what you are selling so you won't be losing money.

The computation of real estate taxes varies considerably from one community to another. The amount of taxes varies, too, depending upon the community and the location of the property. The greater percentage of your property taxes will be for public school purposes, no matter where the property is located. In addition, certain city taxes are received to finance activities for the good of all the people —fire and police protection, street improvements, new sewers, water lines, libraries, and other public services. Real estate taxes become first liens against property if they are not paid, and after a time property can be sold to collect these taxes.

Property taxes are computed on the basis of so many dollars per thousand or hundred dollars of valuation. If the property is usually appraised at half its real value and the tax rate is $33 per $1,000 valuation, then a $30,000 home would have an annual tax due of $495. Such taxes are usually paid annually for the past year. Although many agencies may benefit from such taxes, they are usually all paid in one place and at one time in one lump sum by the property owner. Then all the taxes collected are divided according to an agreed-upon ratio to the various agencies supported in this manner.

From time to time cities will make assessments against property owners for paving a street abutting lots on that street. Sewer and water assessments are common when new facilities are constructed. In a sense these become taxes due and in fact again are first liens against the property if not paid.

And finally, don't forget to take into consideration the cost of improvements and repairs to your house when you are budgeting for its payment. You won't have a landlord now to take care of these items for you. The house will be yours, and you will have to pay for its upkeep. Be especially realistic in your family budget, and again, when you become a home owner, expect the unexpected!

Income Tax Considerations for Home-Owning Clergymen

One of the significant advantages for clergymen who receive a house allowance and then buy their own homes is in the tax savings available to them. Unlike other professional people, clergymen can take advantage of a so-called "double deduction" and actually save money by buying rather than renting a house. It works like this.

For income tax purposes a clergyman may exclude from his taxable income the amount of any allowance he receives for housing which is actually used by him for that purpose. For instance, the man who pays at least $200 a month for rent and utilities or the man whose monthly mortgage payment, including interest, insurance, and taxes, is at least $200, and both of whom receive no more than $2,400 annual house allowance (although by law any reasonable amount is permissible), may exclude from their income the entire amount of allowance received. However, if expenses for providing a home are less than the allowance received, the excess is taxable income.

This provision of the income tax code is to be distinguished from the provisions affecting Social Security self-employment taxes due where the allowance or parsonage rental value is included in computing such self-employment tax.

Then, in addition to this income tax exclusion, the clergyman who buys his own house is allowed to make personal deductions from adjusted gross income (if he elects not to use the 10% standard deduction or new minimum standard deduction) for interest paid on his mortgage and taxes paid on his home. If he is renting there is no deduction available from adjusted gross income for this purpose and no additional tax benefit.

All this can make for a pleasant tax savings of several hundred dollars. Men in the 20% tax bracket will save $480 in taxes on a $2,400 house allowance and besides will save substantially on their deductions for interest and taxes paid. The following example is illustrative. Assume four men have equal incomes, exemptions, and deductions under the following circumstances:

	Non-ordained home owner	Clergyman w/parsonage	Clergyman renting	Clergyman home owner
Salary	$ 10,000	$ 7,600	$ 7,600	$ 7,600
House allowance	—0—	—0—	2,400	2,400
Total cash received	$ 10,000	$ 7,600	$ 10,000	$ 10,000
Exclusion from income for house allowance	—0—	—0—	2,400	2,400
	$ 10,000	$ 7,600	$ 7,600	$ 7,600
Five exemptions @ $600	3,000	3,000	3,000	3,000
	$ 7,000	$ 4,600	$ 4,600	$ 4,600
Other deductions— Contributions, etc.	1,000	1,000	1,000	1,000
	$ 6,000	$ 3,600	$ 3,600	$ 3,600
Interest, taxes, etc.	1,100	—0—	—0—	1,100
Taxable income	$ 4,900	$ 3,600	$ 3,600	$ 2,500
Tax due (1965 rates)	$ 791	$ 552	$ 552	$ 370

Consequently many clergymen have been encouraged to buy homes because of the tax advantages peculiarly available to them. Obviously this is an important consideration when clergymen who receive house allowances are debating the values of renting or buying.

Chapter 6

Savings and Investments

One out of every six adults in the United States today owns shares of stock. The number of individual shareholders in 1965 had tripled since 1952 to a record 20,120,000 people. More Americans are investing more money today in savings accounts, securities, and real estate investments than ever before in the history of our country. More funds, trusts, and foundations have more money than they have ever had available for such investments. Total savings, number of investments in shares, values of real estate are at peak levels. In the midst of all this prosperity intelligent investments are essential for families eager to build their estates, enjoy the comforts of today's booming economy, and provide for their children's education and their own retirement. Savings for a new car, a home, or other dreams are prompting millions of people to make investments unlike any other generation has ever done before in this country.

Clergymen, unlike many other professional people, have probably been slower in getting involved in such investments than most others. Perhaps it is the limitations of their incomes, and yet the majority of all shareholders in the United States have incomes under $10,000. Perhaps they have no interest in such business matters. Perhaps they have simply never inquired into the possibilities. But for whatever reasons they may not be participating now, a minister's family should be as concerned about safe and opportune savings and investment plans as anyone else.

Obviously, any investment requires several cautions. You don't just suddenly go out and buy this or that stock. Nor is it simply a matter of deciding to open a savings account or of buying a piece of property. Clergymen, again like most other people, should seek the competent advice of experts who know the situation. And here, again, your banker is the obvious counselor. Or, if you prefer, a stock broker can advise you on securities, and a competent, licensed realtor can give you many suggestions on desirable land investments.

But before you begin all that, there are several matters related to your own family budget which must be decided before you should even consider making such investments.

Several items need to be thoroughly discussed in your weekly family financial huddle. First of all, you should be certain that your present salary is more than adequate for all your basic needs. If it is and you do have extra funds, then you can safely set aside a specific amount for investment purposes.

Secondly, before you make those investments, you should have available an adequate savings account which is your emergency fund, your cushion, your quick source of cash when you need it. Your family spending plan should include a regular contribution to this savings account. Can you manage about 10% of your salary for savings? This is certainly a good beginning. While such accounts do not increase in value, they do earn a satisfactory interest income and they are safe and quick to get at when needed.

If your salary is adequate and your savings are sufficient to meet possible emergencies, only then will you want to consider other investments. Make a thorough study of the various possibilities and alternatives, risks and costs involved. Be certain that any investment you make beyond your savings account is money which you can afford to lose, not that you will lose it, but be prepared to sacrifice it anyway if worse comes to worse. That is, don't count on being able to liquidate this investment in a hurry or even at all for emergency purposes. Investment officials repeatedly warn small investors always to keep a ready supply of cash on hand and never to invest with funds they cannot afford to lose.

And finally, to emphasize what was said before, be sure you have expert advice on what is best for you from attorneys, accountants, bankers, investment brokers, from someone whom you respect and whose financial judgment is sound.

Investments which are desirable for clergymen are numerous. Beginning, then, with savings accounts, for they are a type of investment too, here are a few suggestions.

Savings Accounts

If you are supporting a growing family, you may always have thought that a savings plan was impossible even for emergency needs. Obviously there are tremendous financial pressures on any young minister and his family. Too often any attempt at a systematic savings plan is considered a luxury which must wait for a more adequate increase in salary, simply because right now there are more pressing needs and bills that must be paid. But if you take a serious view of your family's future and if you intelligently and systematically reorganize your family's spending plan, you will soon become aware of the necessity for saving regularly, and you will discover possibilities for doing it.

Ready cash should be available for emergencies, and a savings account is a far better place for such funds than a cookie jar or even a checking account. When you invest that money you are less likely or able to spend it on current expenses—although in a savings account it is readily available for emergencies—and in the meantime it will be earning interest.

Saving for a college education for your children becomes a near necessity with today's rising tuition and board and room costs in every public and private college. The sooner you begin such a plan, the more money you will have available when you need it some few years hence.

If you need a more rigid compulsion for saving for such an educational fund for your children, you might explore the possibilities of an insurance plan which requires a regular annual payment to accumulate a specified sum by college age, and at the same time provides life insurance coverage for the family's breadwinner.

Of course, there are other objectives for having a savings program. Perhaps you need a down payment for a home, or a new automobile, or a dream fund to challenge your imagination. When you cannot afford the luxury of buying large appliances on time, but can discipline yourself to a regular program of savings, those dreams have a way of coming true and usually at less cost and worry than if you were to buy them all now and pay for them later.

Savings accounts are available at many banks, savings and loan institutions, credit unions, and elsewhere. Interest rates, insured deposits, and ease of withdrawal vary, however, and ought to be clearly understood before you make any commitments.

Savings and loan institutions, which do not offer checking facilities but are essentially loan agencies, will usually offer the greatest amount of earnings, currently between 4% and 5% annually, often compounded quarterly. State and national banks, which in addition offer a variety of banking services, are limited by state and national banking regulations to a maximum rate of interest which they may offer on savings accounts. This amount quite understandably is usually less than that of savings and loan institutions. Credit union and other funds offer satisfactory returns as well, but these accounts are not insured. Savings in the types of banking institutions mentioned offer the most convenient, quick withdrawal procedures, insured savings, and assured return on investment that you can possibly find.

Look for the Federal Deposit Insurance Corporation or Federal Savings and Loan Insurance Corporation membership listing at the institution where you plan to make your savings deposits. At virtually every state bank and in all national banks each depositor is insured by the F.D.I.C. for up to $10,000. Deposits of up to $10,000 in savings and loan institutions are likewise insured, but by the F.S.L.I.C.[1]

Such insurance coverage simply means, as explained in a previous chapter, that any deposits you have in this bank or institution are covered against any loss which might prevent your being paid your full balance on request. If the bank or savings and loan institution should be unable to meet its obligations and thus be forced to close, each depositor will nevertheless receive the entire amount on deposit in all of his accounts up to a maximum of $10,000.

A husband and wife can protect their savings which are in the same bank or institution up to $30,000 by each having individual accounts, as well as a joint account, of $10,000 each. As with checking accounts, so with any bank account, these instrumentalities of the Federal Government established in 1934 are your protection against the devastating effects of a nation-wide lack of confidence in the banks' or institutions' ability to pay depositors, with a resulting run on the bank. This happened once, not so very long ago. While few young men in this generation under age 40 are very much concerned about a repetition of that most recent depression, simply because they were too young then to comprehend it and cannot really imagine such a possibility in today's kind of society, this kind of insurance protection is nevertheless important. Such protection is also important in those rare instances where banks or savings and loan associations fail due to embezzlements, poor management, or for other reasons. You will want to be certain that your deposits are amply protected.

How much you plan to save, of course, is a matter which you must decide. But a specific amount regularly invested is the best plan. Decide upon an amount and then discipline yourself to meet this commitment each month. If it is possible to set aside the 10% mentioned earlier, this would be commendable. Or if you choose a lesser

---

[1]"An act passed on September 21, 1950 . . . made the F.S.L.I.C. insurance payout provision identical to the F.D.I.C.'s. Under this act the F.S.L.I.C. must either pay off an insured account in cash or make available a savings account in the same amount in another insured institution." *1965 Savings and Loan Fact Book,* p. 122.

or greater amount, the important thing is to get started now with a regular contribution so that your fund begins to accumulate and your family gets used to the routine and discipline necessary to carry out this program.

By saving $20 a month, invested at 4%, compounded quarterly, you can accumulate $1,329.95 in five years, $2,952.74 in ten years, $7,348.96 in twenty years. The following chart illustrates the significant amounts which can be accumulated through regular monthly deposits in an account which compounds interest at 4% quarterly.

ACCUMULATION OF SAVINGS WITH REGULAR MONTHLY DEPOSIT (4% Quarterly)

	$5 monthly	$10 monthly	$20 monthly	$25 monthly	$50 monthly
2 years	$ 125.11	$ 250.23	$ 500.45	$ 625.57	$ 1,251.14
5 years	332.49	664.97	1,329.95	1,662.43	3,324.87
10 years	738.18	1,476.37	2,952.74	3,690.92	7,381.84
20 years	1,837.24	3,674.48	7,348.96	9,186.20	18,372.40

Customary procedures for opening savings accounts and making deposits, including cautions with respect to joint accounts in your state, are very similar to those for checking accounts as described in Chapter 2. Withdrawals can usually be made by signing a withdrawal request form or by writing a letter. While there may be a thirty-day waiting period at the option of the bank or savings and loan association, chances are you can have your money any day you request it.

Many savings and loan institutions now pay dividends at the end of each three months, but then usually only on the amounts remaining in the account at the end of that period. Frequently deposits made during the earning period which are received before the tenth of the month receive earnings for the entire month, although this may vary from state to state. Withdrawals during the earning period earn no dividend during that period even if the amounts are kept in the account up to near the end of the period. In other words, if a divident is declared quarterly, amounts deposited by the 10th of January, 10th of February, or 10th of March earn for 3, 2, or 1 months respectively. Amounts withdrawn any time during this period, even toward the end of the third month, earn nothing for the period. Especially large withdrawals, therefore, should be carefully planned to avoid loss of dividend income. Likewise, deposits should be planned to take advantage of these procedures. Even so, some institutions have started computing earnings by the day, so that depositors earn dividends for each day their money is in their account no matter how late in the month such deposits are made. And what has been stated here for savings and loan institutions with respect to payment of dividends usually applies to the payment of interest by banks also.

Explanation should be made here that technically interest is earned only at banks, while dividends are earned at savings and loan institutions. An individual makes deposits in a withdrawable savings (pass book account) or investment account of a savings and loan institution and receives dividends. These dividends are not guaranteed as is interest at a bank, but are periodically declared as payable following the earnings period. A bank, on the other hand, accepts savings deposits and pays interest on these deposits. Savings pass book accounts, savings certificates, and certificates of deposit are possible savings programs for a bank. The latter two arrangements require funds to remain on deposit for longer periods of time but earn a higher rate of interest.[2]

Therefore, while a variety of possibilities exist for maintaining savings accounts, in whatever kind of institution they are made— banks or savings and loan associations—they can be very safe investments which will yield a specific amount of income for you each year. You cannot lose any money on your investment, but at the same time your investment will not grow except by the amount of

---

[2]For income tax purposes such dividends from savings and loan institutions must be reported by the institution to the individual on Form 1099 as interest. The individual taxpayer reports such dividends on Form 1040 as interest income not subject to dividend credit. The institution then deducts such dividends on withdrawable accounts on its own tax return as though it was interest expense. But technically it is still dividend income.

its earnings and the contributions you make to it. Savings do not increase in value. Their dollar amount is the same today as it will be twenty years from now. However, this kind of safe investment is nevertheless a very important investment. The clergyman and his family should give serious consideration to immediate involvement in an accumulation of savings in this manner.

Stocks and Bonds

The warning sounded at the beginning of this chapter is a good rule of thumb to follow before you make any investment beyond a savings account: Don't buy stocks or bonds or make other investments with funds that you cannot afford to lose. That is, you should have readily available funds that will take care of your emergency needs. Of course, you don't expect to lose money on your investments, but you can. The average clergyman is certainly not an expert on investments and furthermore must be quite careful how he uses the funds he does have available.

When you have decided that you would like to make some investments, purchase some stock, or invest in some real estate, you will want to seek the advice of experts before you take the plunge—stockbrokers, real estate agents, bankers. After you have gained some experience, you may trust your own wisdom, but even those who invest regularly often seek the advice of professionals. The clergyman will be more certain in his decisions to buy and sell if he will depend on those who know the business far better than he.

Certainly the clergyman who is interested in making investments ought to become familiar with the terminology, possibilities for investing, and the general field of finance. There is a wealth of information in hundreds of books and pamphlets on the subject. In the next few paragraphs, therefore, the clergyman is simply introduced to a few facts in this field in order to whet the interested man's appetite for this fascinating subject.

Securities are usually classified simply as stocks and bonds. Bonds are issued by various types of organizations: private corporations, utility companies, colleges and universities, cities, states, counties, school districts, the U.S. Government. Public or municipal bonds are usually sold to finance some public works project—a new street, a sewer project, a water works. The U.S. Government issues its familiar savings bonds to finance its work also. Corporations organized for profit-making purposes issue bonds to raise capital (cash) for plant expansion, inventory purchases, etc., without increasing their outstanding stock.

Unlike preferred or common stocks, bonds are a liability for the issuing corporation and become due and payable at a specific time indicated on the bond certificate. Furthermore, bonds earn a precise amount of interest and this is due and payable at specific times regardless of whether the company makes a profit or not. This is an expense, a liability, the company assumes when it sells bonds.

The interest rate of a bond is specified on the certificate. It may be any amount, of course—2%, 5%, 6%—but whatever the amount, this is really what determines its value and consequently the market price for the bond. Bonds, as such, do not increase in value. On their due date the holder will receive the face value, no more, no less. And interest will be paid exactly as shown. A $1,000, 6% bond will earn exactly $60 a year.

Therefore, if you should decide to purchase that $1,000, 6% bond, you might actually pay more or less than $1,000, depending on the effective rate of return you wish to receive from your investment and the length of time until the bond is paid off and redeemed. So that if you paid $1,100 for that bond, you would still receive only $60 a year interest. This would then be equivalent to a 4.5% return or yield on your investment. If you could have purchased the bond at a discount, at less than $1,000, then your rate of return would have been more than the 6% being paid on the bond. Obviously, the actual rate of interest and the effective rate of return are not always the same on your bond investments. Bonds are like savings accounts in that they regularly pay the same amount of interest.

There is, of course, a certain risk involved in purchasing bonds just as there is in most any investment. If the issuing company is forced into liquidating its assets, bond-holders may not get the full value of their investment even though they will receive a distributive share prior to shareholders. The risk, however, is less than with stocks, and therefore the purchase of bonds is often more attractive than of stocks.

Another factor to be considered in the purchase of bonds is the income tax exclusion status of income earned from bonds of a state, city, or other political subdivision. By law, no one is required to pay income taxes on such interest. U.S. Government bond interest and corporation bond interest, however is taxable.

Provisions included in bond issues vary and these should be checked carefully. Some bonds are callable at any time and must be surrendered when called. Some bonds are secured by first mortgages, others by nothing more than the reputation and good name of the issuing corporation. Some bonds are protected by separate instruments requiring reserve or sinking funds which guarantee the eventual accumulation of sufficient funds to pay off the bond indebtedness.

Bonds are not usually sold or purchased as readily or as often as other types of securities, although there is, of course, speculation in them as there is with stocks. For they are certainly marketable and you can determine the current prices and yields, as well as other information on many of them, simply by reading the financial market section of the larger city newspapers. As a matter of fact, bonds are often a good, safe income-producing investment.

Stocks, on the other hand, are different from bonds in many respects. In the first place, they are not the same kind of legal liability for the issuing company. Stocks are considered capital, not liabilities. They do not come due at a particular time, although some are callable. They are, rather, the evidence of one's ownership or investment in the business. Shares are issued to raise money to provide funds for expansion, buildings, other investments, much like the purpose for bonds; but stock purchasers become legal part-owners of the business and are willing to risk a certain amount of funds for the privilege of being an owner. Bondholders have no share in the business management and must eventually give up their bonds to the company. But once you buy a share of stock, you have a certain share in management, depending on the circumstances; and you do not have to sell your security until you so desire, unless there is a merger or other legal requirement for doing so.

Furthermore, unlike bonds, stocks grow or decline in value, and their worth determines the prices for which they are sold and purchased on the open market. Value depends on many things, but primarily on the rate of return experienced, earnings per share, the stability and future prospects of the corporation, and the general market outlook at any particular time.

Some types of shares do include a guaranteed rate of return if earnings are available or profits are made. These are often called preferred stocks, preferred because dividends are guaranteed and paid to these holders according to the rate listed on the certificates before common shareholders receive any distribution. Common shareholders, on the other hand, are not guaranteed any dividends. Nevertheless, common shares often earn a very good rate of return. Their popularity rests in the advantages of their increase in value and their usually ready marketability.

Successful investors reap their rewards from increases in the value of their common stocks and not necessarily because of the earnings on the stock. Growth stocks, those that increase in value, and earnings stocks, those with substantial rates of return and little growth prospect, are purchased for different reasons and result in different types of income to the investor. You should purchase the type that best accomplishes your immediate and long-term investment goals.

Preferred shareholders usually do not have voting rights. Common shareholders, on the other hand, are those who have a voice in the affairs of the corporation, largely because of the greater risk and the lesser assurance of dividends. They do have a voice in the management by being able to elect the directors of their choice to the Board and in a general way to influence the direction in which the policies of the company will go. But all shareholders, whether preferred or common, and no matter how many shares they own, are part-owners of the company.

All shares can earn dividends. In fact, some have guaranteed returns. But the directors of the company determine how much, if any, of the net income will be paid for dividends after all expenses have been met, including bond interest and taxes. Many items influence this decision—how much the company has earned, how much will be used for future expansion, cash funds available for meeting anticipated expenses, and other items.

The amount of dividend paid for each share is not nearly as important as the earnings per share and the yield or rate of return on the investment. Every share of a corporation within the same classification is entitled to the same amount of dividend no matter how much the stock cost the purchaser. And because the value of shares fluctuates almost daily, no two shareholders are likely to pay the same price or enjoy exactly the same rate of return on their investment. A $5 dividend to a shareholder who paid $100 for a share represents a 5% return on the investment. The same share purchased for $75 will receive a $5 dividend also, but the rate of return will be 6.7%. The indicated yield for any stock can be calculated by dividing the sum of cash dividends paid during the past twelve months by the current market price of that stock. Percentages thus become more important than dollar amounts in computing the income which can be anticipated from specific shares.

The price you pay for a share of stock is determined by many factors. "Some are keyed directly to the corporation—its earnings, dividends, management, outlook. Others (and at times these may prove the overriding factors) are national and even international in scope and origin and may have no specific connection with your company. But these factors together make up a stock market. An individual's decision to buy or sell a stock reflects his or her evaluation of its attraction in relation to his or her financial requirements. And these price opinions are registered hour-by-hour, day-by-day in the prices at which stocks are bought and sold.

"A listed corporation has just so many shares outstanding. When you buy shares of any stock on the [New York] Exchange, you must buy from someone else. When you sell, you find someone who wants to buy your shares. The Exchange provides the market place. Buyers compete for the lowest price; sellers compete for the highest price. The Stock Exchange sees that prices are arrived at fairly, openly and published promptly."[3]

Buying and selling securities is a rather simple process once you have made a decision on what you intend to buy or sell. Through brokers located in almost every larger city of our nation, individuals can buy and sell any listed security with no more trouble than it takes to pick up a phone and dial the broker's business number. But behind that decision to buy or sell there should have gone considerable study and planning.

In a recent newspaper advertisement, the New York Stock Exchange offered the following suggestions for would-be investors:

"Guide #1: Keep a cool head about hot rumors. Maybe you're next on the list of a tipster. He might be a stranger on the phone, or even a friend who thinks he's doing you a favor, calling you with so-called inside information on a stock that's about to take off. The jargon of the tipster can have an appealing ring. But there's no wiser guide to smart investing than to apply a cool head to cool facts. And to be wary of any rumor marked 'rush.'

"Guide #2: Understand what a Member Firm broker can do for you. He's a good man to turn to when you dig for facts. If you should become interested in a particular company, ask him for information about it. Perhaps he can get you an annual report. Discuss its reported earnings, dividend record and plans. It may be important to get his opinion on how it stands in its field and what

---

[3]*Investment Facts,* published by the New York Stock Exchange, Nov. 1964, New York, N.Y., p. 6.

he thinks of its prospects. There's risk in any investment, so invite his opinions on that point too. (But don't expect that he will always be right.) Then bring your own judgment to bear. Finally, if you decide to invest, he will have your order executed and send you a confirmation.

"Guide #3: Know your broker's qualifications. Member Firms of the New York Stock Exchange are subject to many qualifying standards and a wide range of Exchange rules, including surprise audits. In addition, every Registered Representative has had to meet the Exchange's requirements for knowledge of his business at the time he became a broker in a Member Firm. He's not infallible, but his point of view can help season your own judgment.

"Guide #4: Before you decide, review your goal. A stock that's right for one person might miss the mark for you. Your need may be to build a second income—from dividends on stock or interest from bonds—or to give your stock a chance to grow in value over a span of years. Possibly you prefer bonds for the greater safety of principal and stability of income they frequently offer.

"Guide #5: Consider carefully how much you might invest. The aim of investing, of course, is to improve your financial position. But the smart investor takes that step only after providing first for living expenses and emergencies."[4]

Of course, the New York Stock Exchange is not the only stock exchange, and you may wish to make investments through other brokers. However, these suggestions are applicable wherever and whenever you expect to make such investments.

One of the most desirable types of investments which the author has found and which is extremely suitable to the beginning and modest investments of a clergyman, is one of the various mutual funds. Such investments are not very speculative and yet provide one of the safest and most systematic methods of improving your financial position.

---

[4]*Six Guides to Smart Investing,* advertisement of the New York Stock Exchange in the *Houston Chronicle,* Houston, Texas, October 10, 1964.

Mutual funds are really companies whose business is the ownership of securities in other companies. They manufacture and sell nothing. The dividends they pay represent their earnings from all the various stocks and bonds they own. Their increase in value represents the overall increase in value of the securities included in their portfolios. As a shareholder in a mutual fund, you have no real decision about what stocks are bought or sold by the company. Furthermore, you pay a higher than usual counseling fee for the administration of the fund, but then you have none of the worries involved in making decisions as to which stocks are most desirable. Then, too, when you buy or sell such securities, the commission or "loading factor" is usually higher than a broker's fee. While the history of mutuals has indicated a much slower growth in appreciation of shares, nevertheless the growth factor has been present and, along with the income available through dividends, these plans provide a very attractive type of investment for clergymen who are just beginning to make investments.

Of course, you can purchase any kind and any amount of shares you can afford. A sudden windfall, prize money, an inheritance, can be invested in any security you choose. A well-known investment counseling firm offers the following suggestion:

"Most professional investors (institutions) want to own only the best quality companies because they expect them to be the most successful in the long run. This has been one of the key factors causing the generally higher level of price-earnings ratios[5] on 'blue chip' stocks since the mid-1950's.

"The institutional impact is also important in a bear market (prices generally decrease in a 'bear market,' increase in a 'bull market') when good stocks may drop just as fast as low-grade ones. During a general decline the institutions are not likely to be selling stocks but they do tend to hold down on their buying. However, as prices become more attractive, they start to make purchases.

---

[5]The ratio of the market value of a stock to its current annual earnings. A high ratio may indicate overpricing and a low ratio possible underpricing.

"This is particularly important in periods of stress such as 1962. The demand for stocks then stems almost entirely from professionals and their clients, and they are interested only in the better-grade issues. So there is always demand for good stocks. In times like that 'the public' has long since lost interest and there is no one left to buy the 'cats and dogs.' As a result, the best-quality issues receive buying support earlier and recover faster.

"These are some of the reasons why the individual investor should be interested primarily in the institutional-grade stocks. It is the holders of such issues who are most certain to have successful investment results over the longer term."[6]

Investing large sums of money in securities all at one time is generally not possible for most clergymen. A few years ago the New York Stock Exchange initiated a plan called the Monthly Investment Plan, MIP, whereby investors could buy stock out of income with payments as small as $40 quarterly up to $1,000 monthly.

"MIP sets up a regular program—a good habit in savings or buying securities. As you invest the same number of dollars periodically, say each month or quarter, your payment buys more stock when the price is low and less when it is high. . . . All the bookkeeping is done for you. After every purchase you make, you'll receive a confirmation showing the amount received, number of full shares and/or fractional shares in your account, odd lot price paid, commission charged and a reminder of the date your next payment is due.

"More than 7½ million shares of stock have been purchased under the Plan since it was introduced in 1954. The dozen companies most popular with MIP investors are: General Motors Corp., American Tel. & Tel. Co., International Business Machines Corp., General Tel. & Electronics Corp., Tri-Continental Corp., Minnesota Mining and Mfg. Co., General Electric Co., Standard Oil Co. (N.J.), Dow Chemical Co., Pfizer (Charles) & Co., Inc., Radio Corp. of Amer-

---

[6]*Weekly Staff Letter,* David L. Babson and Company, Incorporated, 89 Broad Street, Boston, Mass., Monday, May 31, 1965.

ica, and Sears Roebuck Co., Inc."[7] For payments of less than $100 you pay a 6% commission for the service. As the payment increases, the percentage goes down.

The benefit of such a plan gradually accrues to the faithful and systematic investor. Over a period of time the value of those purchases may increase substantially over the original purchase price if the general economy is advancing. As explained, investors in the MIP or similar plans will eventually average out the highs and lows in their investments and over the long run improve their financial situation.

No matter which plan is followed, the wise investor will keep informed of the progress of the securities he owns. This means he will have to be able to read stock market reports, comprehend the Dow-Jones industrial and commodities reports, understand financial statements published by "his company," and in general be somewhat familiar with financial terminology. Even though most clergymen are grossily uninformed in these areas, they can quickly learn enough to be at least familiar with the processes while still depending upon the experts to provide the significant information necessary to make intelligent decisions.

Many of the large city newspapers provide daily reports on all activities related to all securities listed on the various national stock exchanges. For most clergymen the financial pages are a veritable jungle of unintelligible fine print statistics involving endless columns of abbreviations and mysterious symbols. Actually, this is the very heart of the securities business, and a reading knowledge of these pages could be most helpful if you are interested in such investments.

Various reports are available on American Stock Exchange quotations, New York Stock Exchange quotations, mutual funds, treasury bonds, other bond transactions, earnings reports, and so forth. A typical line in the *Houston Post,* for instance, of Nov. 29, 1964, under the American Stock Exchange quotation for the Viewlex Company, famous for their slide and filmstrip projectors, reads: "5⅜ 3 Viewlex

---

[7]*Investment Facts, op. cit.,* pp. 8-9.

35 4⅝ 4¼ 4¼ -⅜." Briefly this means that the highest and lowest prices paid thus far in 1964 for one share has been $5.375 and $3.00 respectively. On this particular day of trading 3,500 shares were involved in buying and selling transactions with the highest price paid per share today of $4.625 and the lowest price of $4.25 per share. The low price happened to be the closing price for the day. The net change in price for the day was a $.375 drop.

Among mutual funds on this particular day, as reported by the National Association of Securities Dealers, Inc., Keystone Custodian Funds Hi-Grade Common Series S-1 could have sold for a high of $25.86 per share, a low of $25.80 per share, and closed for the day at $25.82, compared to a closing price the previous week of $25.84.

A variety of publications are available which will give you a considerable amount of information about industry trends, corporate dividends and earnings, and market patterns. Ask your local broker for suggestions for a worthwhile, interesting publication using down-to-earth language. Here is fascinating reading you will really enjoy if you are interested in the stock market.

U.S. Government Savings Bonds Series E

Another excellent type of investment is Series E U.S. Government savings bonds. The popularity of this type of savings has waned considerably since the end of World War II, but the bonds are still available and at even higher rates of interest than before. They are still backed by the credit of the U.S. and are therefore one of the best investments anywhere in the world. With a Series E savings bond you are assured of interest earnings and the return of all your capital investment. Furthermore, should you desire to do so, you can cash in your bonds at any time after the initial waiting period (30-60 days) and receive your entire cash investment plus any accumulated interest. No advance notice is necessary, and you can cash bonds at many convenient locations.

The rate of return on such bonds varies, however, depending upon the purchase date and the length of time the bond is held. Series E bonds were first issued in 1941 with a ten-year maturity date, and when held to maturity earned 2.9%. While the redemption value of the bonds has remained the same ever since—$25 for an $18.75 bond— the Federal Government has shortened the time to maturity to 7 years for bonds purchased after December 1, 1965. This increases the net yield to 4.15% and makes the bonds more attractive to prospective purchasers and more competitive with other types of savings accounts. These bonds if held beyond maturity continue to earn 4.15% for up to an additional ten years.

Series E savings bonds are issued in the following maturity value denominations: $25, $50, $75, $100, $500, $1,000, $10,000. Only the owner or his heir or beneficiary may redeem the bond. Such bonds are not negotiable and cannot be used for collateral.

The following table shows the cash redemption value of a $100 bond from issue date to maturity for bonds bearing an issue date after December 1, 1965:

Period held after issue date	Redemption value during each half-year period
First ½ year	$ 75.00
½ to 1 year	75.84
1 to 1½ years	77.28
1½ to 2 years	78.80
2 to 2½ years	80.40
2½ to 3 years	82.08
3 to 3½ years	83.84
3½ to 4 years	85.68
4 to 4½ years	87.56
4½ to 5 years	89.48
5 to 5½ years	91.44
5½ to 6 years	93.44
6 to 6½ years	95.52
6½ to 7 years	97.68
Maturity value (7 years from issue date)	$ 100.00

Other Investments

If your interest extends beyond savings, stocks, and bonds, you may find opportunity to spend your extra dollars for other types of investments. These could involve a variety of enterprises limited only by your money and your ingenuity—investments in small businesses, rental property, inventions, farm and ranch lands, business property, and so forth.

Such investments will likely involve considerably more risk than investments previously discussed—and more time. And they will generally require a much more careful investigation. The advice of experts becomes even more critical when these kinds of investments are being considered. Of course, the investor will need to be more informed and knowledgeable about the venture also.

While many possibilities are available, here are a few suggestions. If you are considering rental property, you will need to be familiar with many of the items discussed in the chapter on buying a home. Whether you buy a home, a duplex, or an apartment, several important matters beyond those considered previously must be studied.

For instance, what is the rental, and what rate of return can be expected on your investment? Is there a demand for rental units like this? What major repairs are necessary? Is the property likely to increase in value? Will you be able to maintain the property yourself, or will you need to turn the matter over to a realtor for rental, collection, and maintenance? What are the other risks? How difficult will selling this property be if that becomes necessary? Are there income tax considerations that are beneficial or detrimental to you in this situation?

Buy a farm or a ranch and you have similar problems—cost, anticipated income, future value, rate of return on investment, and so forth. Unimproved real property held for investment or sale must also be carefully selected. What is the current appraised value? Are taxes high? What use is made of adjoining properties? Are there deed or zoning restrictions? What type of building or business is likely to be built or located on this site? Are railroads, highways, throughways, water, electricity, gas, available if needed? What limitations are included in city building codes? Are new roads or other easements likely to make the property less valuable in the future—and so forth.

Summary

While investments are desirable for families with cash available for that purpose, in addition to their savings for emergencies and current needs, considerable care and judgment must be exercised for a successful venture. Most important, be sure that your family's needs are taken care of first through a savings plan before you launch out on some speculative investment spree. And then, don't buy until you have evaluated the advice and opinion of experts in this field. Their advice may not be free, but it is inexpensive and valuable. Don't take a chance with your family's money. Know what the risks are, and be as safe as you can whenever you take the giant step toward investing.

Chapter 7

Retirement Planning

Providing a comfortable retirement is no longer the problem it used to be for clergymen. Today's tremendous upsurge in retirement apartments, hotel complexes for the well-elderly, and indeed whole cities where a condition for home ownership is a minimum age of 60 or 65, make the selection of a retirement home much easier than it used to be. Increased salaries, adequate pension plans, intelligent investments, and Social Security have all contributed substantially to the retirement benefits of today's clergymen. Indeed, the entire nation is becoming increasingly conscious of its "senior citizens." It is probably easier and more rewarding to be "older" today than it was a generation ago.

Today there are more people than ever before who are over 65. Within the next ten years, in one state of the nation alone, it is estimated that there will be 40% more persons over age 65 than there are today. Retired ministers will be able to take just as much advantage of the additional income possibilities and housing provisions for the elderly as anyone else.

Furthermore, retirement pension benefits, not only for ministers, but for all workers, continually increase. New programs, more liberal provisions, greater employer pension fund contributions and fringe benefit arrangements, all contribute to a more enjoyable retirement life. In recent years church denominations have vastly extended the benefits available to ministers, and more changes will inevitably be made. And of course the provisions of Social Security bring additional sources of income for many clergymen.

113

In fact, there are several possible sources of retirement income available for clergymen: church denomination retirement plans, or Social Security, or income-producing investments such as real estate, annuities, businesses, stocks, and bonds. Most clergymen will have access to the first two and many may have opportunity to explore the possibilities in some area of the third.

By the mid-1960's most of the larger denominations in the nation had provided some kind of pension program for their clergymen, even though these plans varied considerably in their scope and coverage. Nevertheless, most denominations continue to make every effort to improve their pension benefits and thus to narrow the gap between active salaries and retirement payments. In fact, many denominations are making notable exceptions for their older retirees by granting greater benefits than would normally be permitted on the basis of the individual's contributions to the fund over the past years. There is a growing awareness in the church that retired pastors who never had the opportunity to contribute more, simply because the plans were not then in existence, should nevertheless be given increased benefits to make their retirement years more enjoyable.

No two plans, of course, require the same contributions or payments or grant the same benefits. One denomination requires its members to contribute annually at least 4% of their salary while the congregation or salary-paying organizations are required to contribute at least 8%. Another denomination requires the entire 12% contribution to be paid by the congregation. And other denominations have different plans. Most of the plans provide for additional contributions above the minimum, thus providing greater benefits at retirement. In addition, interest accumulations, usually at 4%, add to the final benefit amounts. Your own denomination's pension board will be glad to send you additional information about your specific benefits. If during your active ministry you have faithfully contributed the minimum amount required, your retirement income may very well nearly equal the average annual salary you have received during your entire ministry. Obviously, this may be considerably less than your salary just before retirement, but it is likely to be substantially more than has ever been available to retired ministers before.

Several income tax considerations become important in connection with pension programs, and you should inquire from an accountant about those provisions directly affecting you. One such immediate tax benefit affects the payments you are now making through payroll deductions to your pension plan. Under the present regulation you can exclude from your taxable income the amount of your pension contributions withheld from your salary. Any income tax which you may ever pay on these amounts will be due only when you begin receiving your retirement income. At that time, it is assumed that your tax bracket will likely be less on account of lowered income and greater deductions. Obviously, this is not a tax exemption, but a tax deferment. Inquire at your pension board headquarters for further and more explicit details on this matter.

Whenever you retire your pension board will calculate for you, based on your own contributions to the fund and those made on your behalf, the amount of monthly pension which you will receive for the rest of your life. And, unless your denomination votes at some future time to increase the payment, that is the amount you will receive, no matter what other sources of retirement income you may have.

A second type of retirement income available to clergymen is Social Security. This is both an insurance program, as explained in Chapter 4, and a retirement program. The plan provides for retirement payments beginning at age 62 for men and women covered under Social Security. It also provides disability, survivors', and death benefit payments under the insurance portion of the program. The amount of benefits you may receive will depend upon your average taxable salary as computed for Social Security purposes during the years prior to your retirement. The actual amount which you contribute is not significant in this respect. The exact amount of benefit payments which you will receive cannot be determined, however, until the time you actually file your claim at retirement age. Present regulations, as amended in 1965, permit the benefit payments as shown in the chart below.

EXAMPLES OF MONTHLY SOCIAL SECURITY CASH BENEFIT PAYMENTS[1]

Average yearly earnings after 1950	$3,600	$4,800	$6,600
Retirement at 65/Disability benefits	$ 112.40	$ 135.90	$ 168.00
Retirement at 64	105.00	126.90	156.80
Retirement at 63	97.50	117.80	145.60
Retirement at 62	90.00	108.80	134.40
Wife's benefit at 65 or with child in her care	56.20	68.00	84.00
Wife's benefit at 64	51.60	62.40	77.00
Wife's benefit at 63	46.90	56.70	70.00
Wife's benefit at 62	42.20	51.00	63.00
One child of retired or disabled worker	56.20	68.00	84.00
Widow age 62 or over	92.80	112.20	138.60
Widow at 60, no child	80.50	97.30	120.20
Widow under 62 and 1 child	168.60	204.00	252.00
Widow under 62 and 2 children	240.00	306.00	368.00
One surviving child	84.30	102.00	126.00
Two surviving children	168.60	204.00	252.00
Maximum family payment	240.00	309.20	368.00
Lump-sum death payment	255.00	255.00	255.00

Generally, in figuring average yearly earnings after 1950, 5 years of low earnings or no earnings can be excluded. The maximum earnings creditable for Social Security are $3,600 for 1951-54; $4,200 for 1955-58; $4,800 for 1959-65; and $6,600 starting in 1966. Because of this, the benefits shown in the last column will not generally be payable for some years to come. When a person is entitled to more than one benefit, the amount actually payable is limited to the largest of the benefits.

By writing to the Social Security Administration offices in Baltimore, Maryland, on a form available at your local Social Security office [Form OAR-7004 (12-64)], you can secure specific information which shows your recorded earnings on your Social Security account. On the basis of this information, you may be able to estimate the benefits which will be available to you upon retirement.

[1] *Social Security Amendments 1965, A Brief Explanation,* U.S. Department of Health, Education, and Welfare, Social Security Administration, OASI-1965-1, GPO: 1965 0-784-861, August, 1965, 3rd ed.

However, your benefits may be reduced during retirement up to age 72 if you receive income from part-time work in excess of $1,500 annually. Your benefits will be reduced by approximately $1 for each $2 of earnings over $1,500 which you receive. However, no benefits will be withheld in any month when your other income does not exceed $125. If you are receiving Social Security benefits, therefore, it is important that you keep accurate records of your earnings month by month.

However, not all income is necessarily included in this $1,500 annual limit. For instance, income from interest or dividends or retirement programs may not result in any reduction in Social Security benefits. Reimbursed expenses for operating an automobile on church business are not included. And as the tax laws of the nation are changed from time to time, other items may be included or excluded. Considerable care, therefore, needs to be taken to be certain that outside income will not jeopardize monthly Social Security payments.

Ordained clergymen, however, are not automatically eligible to receive the benefits listed on the previous page. Men in the program now and those who are receiving benefits have elected to be covered by filing waiver form #2031 with the Internal Revenue Service.

All clergymen had the opportunity to make this election several years ago when Social Security was first made available to them. The election, however, had to be made within a certain period and therefore, prior to the passage of the 1965 amendments to the Social Security Act, time for election had run out for many ministers.

Prior to April 15, 1966, ordained men were given one more opportunity to elect coverage under Social Security and pay, by that date, all taxes due beginning with 1963. Because the 1965 legislation added many new benefits to the program, especially Medicare and increased retirement benefits, many clergymen previously not involved have now elected to take advantage of the opportunity to enroll.

Recently-ordained ministers may still enroll, since men on a calendar year tax basis have until April 15 of the year following the second year in which they had at least $400 taxable income to file the waiver form, pay the self-employment taxes due for the previous eligible years, and thus enroll. Ministers who failed to enroll during their previous allowable time or by April 15, 1966, may not enroll later. Henceforth, under present legislation at least, ministers may enroll only within the previously described two-year time or forever lose the opportunity to participate. Of course, Congress may still provide another chance sometime in the future for ministers to join.

The self-employment tax rate is now set according to the following schedule.

CONTRIBUTION RATE SCHEDULE FOR SELF-EMPLOYED PEOPLE[2]

Years	Maximum taxable salary	Rate for old-age, survivor, & disability insurance benefits	Rate for hospitalization insurance	Total rate	Maximum amount of self-employment tax
1965	$ 4,800	5.40	.00	5.40	$ 259.20
1966	6,600	5.80	.35	6.15	405.90
1967-68	6,600	5.90	.50	6.40	422.40
1969-72	6,600	6.60	.50	7.10	468.60
1973-75	6,600	7.00	.55	7.55	498.30
1976-79	6,600	7.00	.60	7.60	501.60
1980-86	6,600	7.00	.70	7.70	508.20
1987 & after	6,600	7.00	.80	7.80	514.80

Clergymen covered by Social Security file their own annual tax returns as self-employed persons, paying the tax due along with their income taxes each year. The congregation has nothing to do with this.

When computing your self-employment tax, you must include, up to $6,600, your total cash salary plus honorariums, fees, royalties, rental incomes, etc., as well as the rental value of a parsonage furnished you or the actual amount of a house allowance paid to you or on your behalf. You may, of course, deduct allowable expenses,

[2]Ibid.

but it is to your ultimate advantage to pay the maximum tax in order to gain the maximum benefits available at retirement. And, as explained in detail in Chapter 5, even though the rental value of a parsonage or a reasonable house allowance are taxable for Social Security purposes, they are excludable from income for income tax purposes.

And finally, it is important periodically to review the provisions of Social Security to determine what benefits will be available to you whenever you become eligible for them. Write to the Baltimore, Maryland, office of the Social Security Administration and ask for the special booklet explaining Social Security benefits specifically available for clergymen. Familiarize yourself with the current provisions of the law. Your future retirement security depends on intelligent and informed decisions today.

In addition to these two sources of retirement income, income from various investments is also possible. If you have been fortunate enough to accumulate sufficient funds and wish to make prudent investments that will provide an assured retirement income, you may consider some of the following possibilities.

Annuities

The primary purpose of an annuity is to liquidate a principal sum regardless of how that sum came into being. When an annuity is purchased a principal sum is exchanged for a promise to make periodic payments to the annuitant for as long as he lives.

Annuities were created to offset the fear of outliving one's income. "For generations many people have discovered that when they can no longer earn income, their accumulated estates are of insufficient size to generate enough income to sustain them for the balance of their lives. Their only recourse, in many instances, is to dip into principal in order to maintain adequate income. But invading principal immediately creates the beginning of a vicious circle. As the principal is reduced, income from the principal remaining declines, thus requiring more principal which further reduces the yield, thus making it necessary to liquidate principal at an ever-increasing rate. The upshot, of course, is that the owner faces the danger of having his principal expire before he does.

"Through the years, literally millions of people have lived in fear and under the constant threat of outliving their financial resources. The annuity came into being as economic protection against living too long. While all of us want to live a full and useful life, none of us relishes the thought of becoming a financial burden to relatives, or a ward of society. Only the annuity overcomes this basic economic hazard by scientifically utilizing principal together with interest to yield a maximum income that cannot be outlived.

"Thus, the annuity is used primarily by people who want guaranteed income which cannot be outlived."[3] For persons with larger estates, annuities can serve other purposes, too, tailored to fit the particular needs of the people involved. In any instance, if you have the funds available for such a program, on account of a matured endowment insurance policy, or an inheritance, or the sale of property or other investments, it would be well for you to discuss the matter with your banker or attorney.

Annuities are extremely flexible and are written in many ways under varying circumstances to meet different needs. Every annuity, though, no matter how it is created, is an agreement to pay a stipulated sum each month (or at some other regular periodic time) to the annuitant.

Most annuity programs are written with insurance companies. In recent years, however, many people, both of substantial and more modest means, who wish to make a contribution to their favorite charity and yet must retain an income from their estates for the rest of their lives, have entered into agreements with churches, religious foundations, colleges, and other charitable non-profit organizations

---

[3]*The Annuity, Today's Greatest Income Bargain,* prepared and published for Metropolitan Life Insurance Company by the Research & Review Service of America, Inc., Indianapolis, Indiana, 1964, pp. 1-2.

for various types of guaranteed annual income payments. Several plans are available, and if you are interested, inquiry should be made to the organization which you would like to support.

Such institutions offer various life income and annuity plans, all of which provide lifetime income and the opportunity eventually to contribute substantially to the institution. Some of these plans are described below.

The charitable gift annuity is similar to any insurance company annuity in that a specific periodic payment beginning at a specific time is guaranteed for life in exchange for a principal sum. The annuity payment may be less than with an insurance plan, because the charitable gift provision assumes an approximate residual remainder (a gift to the institution) of at least 50% of the original principal amount paid for the annuity agreement. Annuity payments will include both income and a partial return of principal. Based on carefully calculated actuarial statistical information, the annuity is written with this basic assumption in mind. This type of arrangement provides a greater periodic income for the same amount of investment than either of the following plans. But it too has several important income tax considerations which must be carefully evaluated.

A life income contract specifies that the beneficiary will receive for life the average yield produced from the portfolio of the institution's unrestricted investments. The principal sum contributed at the outset will be exactly the amount available to the institution at the beneficiary's death and will then be available for whatever purpose it was originally intended.

A life income trust is a similar arrangement and differs only in that the principal sum contributed is kept in trust and the specific income from this restricted investment, less a modest administration fee, is paid for the lifetime of the donor.

Obviously, there are many alternatives to these various plans, but these few illustrations should give the clergyman some understanding of them. When the time comes for your retirement, choices must be made for the most advantageous use of the resources you have accumulated through a lifetime of service to the church.

Retirement Housing

But retirement involves more, of course, than simply planning for a source of income during the retirement years when regular salary has ceased. Another factor which clergymen especially must consider is that of a home. Since retirement incomes are not exceptionally large in comparison to previous salaries earned, considerable caution must be taken in the spending of whatever funds are available. The selection of a place to live must be done with the utmost care.

Fortunately, this planning is often done early, so that the decision is made long before retirement age is reached. In fact, it can be an extremely discouraging experience to be confronted suddenly at age 65 with the necessity of buying a house when a parsonage has been provided for more than 40 years. Nevertheless, if a home is purchased, certain factors which are unique for retired persons and which are in addition to the usual house-buying concerns must be taken into consideration.

1. Is the cost commensurate with pension income, or will it take too big a slice from available resources? Are there alternatives which can reduce cost—fewer conveniences or a less elaborate arrangement?

2. Is the location favorable? Is it close enough to friends so the elderly won't be lonely or feel left out? Are the children or other relatives reasonably close for periodic visits to the retired? Are hospitals, shopping centers, recreation and entertainment facilities nearby? Are the costs of living in this location commensurate with retirement income?

3. If a house is purchased, is it suitable in size, room arrangement, floor levels, steps, etc., for the elderly? What is its resale value? If it is an older house, is retirement income sufficient for maintenance? What about the availability of utilities, care of the lawn, community responsibilities?

4. If an apartment is rented or purchased in a housing development or condominium specifically for older persons, considerable investigation ought to be made about costs, provisions for leaving, hospital care, use of recreational facilities, meals, entertainment, general attitude of those who already live nearby, costs for extra services in addition to lodging and food, etc.

Other Retirement Considerations

Ministers may also consider other items than those listed above as they make plans for a practical, worthwhile, enjoyable retirement, as free as possible from financial worries. Additional sources of income to supplement pension payments should be investigated. Supply preaching is generally always available. Other church work—visiting the sick in several hospitals in a large city for the benefit of several churches may be possible; assisting some congregation on a part-time basis in various other phases of church work may be arranged. Retirement offers opportunity for writing and publication, perhaps even for lecturing or other speaking engagements. The man who retires to a rural home may find opportunity to raise a few cattle or farm vegetables for the local markets if he is so inclined.

In all these ventures, however, the retired person receiving Social Security payments must be careful that the total income from such sources does not exceed $125 a month, at least until he is 72. For if it does, the monthly benefit check will be reduced proportionately.

The clergyman who begins planning early in his career for retirement has the prospect of realizing a comfortable and enjoyable, even active, life as a senior citizen.

Chapter 8

Wills and Other Legal Documents

So, you are finally sitting down to write your will? Good, for when you do you will no longer be one of those six out of every ten Americans who does not have a will and who has little intention of writing one. At least you have decided to make an intelligent disposition of your assets when you die rather than letting someone else decide for you. At this moment, if you are writing your will, you are taking steps to tell the world what you want done with your estate. You no longer want the State to tell you what will be done with it. You do not want a court to appoint guardians for your children. You do not want someone who has never known you, never lived near you, never cared about you, to administer the affairs of your estate.

When you have finally written your will, you will know for certain that your wife will get what you want her to have. You know your children will be properly cared for by their mother. You know that those friends and relatives you care about will share in your estate just as you want them to. Because you refuse to let the State draw your will for you—as indeed the State has already done for everyone who has no last will and testament—you are about to write out your own will.

This means that you are finally convinced that it isn't necessary to be rich to write a will, that you won't die any sooner on account of it, and that it's really not going to cost you very much after all. If you are already writing your will, you have probably listed your

124

assets and liabilities, evaluated your ambitions for your friends and family, and discussed the whole matter with your wife. You are writing a will, and you are to be congratulated for it!

By now you have probably discussed it all with your attorney too. But you are doing it all yourself, you say? You have the facts handy? You know what you want to do, and this way it won't cost you anything? Well, all right, but why not see your attorney to be sure you have done it all correctly before it's too late to change mistakes?

After all, a family lawyer is really no different from a family doctor, and he can write your will much better for you than you can yourself. You'd never expect to diagnose your own health ailments; at least most of us go to a doctor when we're sick. You'd never trust a chemist to survey real property you have purchased, and you are not likely to pull your own teeth. So take this advice, see your family lawyer now and let him write that will for you before you make a mistake which might nullify the entire will. Then you will be sure that your preferences have been stated correctly and everyone can understand precisely what you want. After you are gone, it will be too late to clarify uncertainties.

Of course, there are some people who do write their own wills, and they get away with it. But the risk is far too great for you to take that kind of gamble, preacher or not! One technical error is enough to throw out the entire will, and then your estate, however modest, is up to the mercy of the courts. And while most of us have few worries about too much money, chances are we have legal problems we are entirely unaware of, things like legal residence and property titles and joint bank accounts and simultaneous deaths. Few clergymen were ever attorneys, but even those who were will quickly suggest that you go see your attorney when you write your will.

If You Do Not Have a Will—

But until you have had that will written, properly signed, and witnessed, you do not have a will, no matter how good your intentions are. And to be without a will has serious consequences. Complications are in store for your relatives if you do not get it done.

Catherine Marshall, wife of the famous Washington, D.C., minister, Peter Marshall, describes her exasperating experiences in dealing with her husband's estate. Peter Marshall did not have a will. "When I discovered the amazing amount of red tape involved even with such a small estate, I almost ran to a lawyer to get help in making a will of my own. Not only that, but I began urging my parents and close friends to consider the same move. Though in my case there was little to leave anyone, I reasoned that the tiny sum involved in making a will might some day save many times that amount in fees for dealing with quite unnecessary legal technicalities."[1]

Or, here was "a young father, owner of a small suburban retail store, killed in an automobile accident on his way home one fogbound night. He left no will. According to the laws of his state, his wife received one-third of his estate, including the small business, while his four young children were given the remainder.

"Because the children were minors, their property became the concern of the court. Since there wasn't enough money in the widow's share to care for all expenses, she was forced to petition the court for some of the children's money. This required her to post a bond, pay court and legal fees. Until the children are of legal age, the widow must continue to be burdened by legal problems and costs involved in periodic reports to the court. It could all have been avoided had her husband left a proper will."[2]

Suppose you have a wife and four minor children, and you die intestate, without a will. You have a house in joint tenancy with your wife. You have $25,000 of life insurance payable to your wife if she survives you, otherwise to your children. You have a car worth $3,000 in your own name, as well as a small savings account and some se-

---

[1]Catherine Marshall, *To Live Again* (Copyright © 1957 McGraw-Hill Book Company, Inc., New York). Used by permission of McGraw-Hill Book Company.

[2]Lester David, *Why You Should Choose a Family Lawyer Now!* New York Life Insurance Co. booklet approved by the American Bar Association, 1964.

curities worth $8,000. Your joint checking account has $750. Remember you have no will. What happens?

Depending upon the state in which you live,[3] this is what may happen. The house, of course, goes to your wife because of the joint ownership; so does the checking account. The proceeds from your insurance policies do, too, because your wife is designated as beneficiary. A will or no will would not affect these three items.

But what about the rest—the car, the savings account, the securities? Who gets them? In order for your wife to look after these items, she will have to have herself appointed administratrix of your estate by the court. But she will have to post bond, and at today's rates that could be expensive.

Still she cannot just take over your assets. She can only administer them. She will sell the car and the securities, close out the savings account, and from the proceeds pay your funeral expenses and other bills left by you. But even then the balance left is not hers to spend as she wants to.

The court will then distribute this amount according to the laws of the state where you lived and died, and these laws will differ from state to state. Your widow may get a third, and your children two-thirds. However, your children's share will be held in trust for them, and if your wife cannot qualify as guardian of their financial affairs, a bank may be appointed to look after these funds until the children are all over twenty-one. Again, the court may have to approve expenditures on behalf of your children no matter who is guardian. And the bank has fees for its services, another cost if you do not have a will.

How much simpler if you have a will! Everything you have can go exactly where you want it to go. You will probably want your wife to have it all anyway, so you will only need to say so in your will and she will get it.

Of course, your wife can be designated by you as executrix and

---

[3]In many states joint ownership of real estate does not automatically remove the property from an estate at death.

guardian, and as soon as your will has been probated she gets your entire estate, and there is no further need to get involved with the courts. While holding everything in joint ownership may solve some problems, it will not solve them all. A will can spell out precisely what you want done, whether your estate is large or small. Your attorney can help you prevent problems for your wife while you are still available to make the decisions and sign a will.

Selecting an Attorney

Which attorney should you go to? You could read through the yellow pages of any telephone directory and take your pick. But don't! Go to your family lawyer first. If you don't have one, now is the best time to get one, before you are in trouble. Even though there may not be many times when you need a lawyer, when you do you probably need him in a hurry. Thumbing through the yellow pages takes time, and besides the lawyer you call may not want to help you just then. A family lawyer will. Choose one now.

Suppose your teen-age son is involved in a car accident at 1:00 A.M. some Saturday night and is charged with a serious traffic violation. If you called your family lawyer right away, he would come. Of course, you would probably be able to get another lawyer eventually. But how much better to have a friend who knows you to help you!

Furthermore, especially when you write your will, a family lawyer (or the trust department of your bank) who is already acquainted with you may be able to give you far better advice than someone else. Of course, even your family lawyer will refer you to another attorney who is a specialist in such matters if there are special or peculiar problems with your estate. After all, there are experts and specialists in the field of law just as in medicine or theology. Your family lawyer, though, will work with the specialists in arranging the best disposition of your estate according to your wishes.

So if you are starting out fresh to find a lawyer who can write your will, you will do best to pick one experienced in wills. He will help you avoid pitfalls, and he will ask you key questions. Perhaps there is such a man in your congregation. Or ask your banker; he will help you find one, too.

But whether it's a lawyer new to you or the one you've used for years in other matters, either will need considerable information before he can write that will for you. Some of what he will want will involve facts about your present financial situation; other items will involve your attitudes and ideas, your plans and ambitions, your hopes and fears. Of course, you can write all this out yourself and intend it for your will, but it may not be a will after all. Better let an attorney help you put it all together as it ought to be done.

Check List for a Will

Here is a check list of items you will need for your will, as adapted from *Changing Times,* The Kiplinger Magazine, May, 1959, issue. Have you got it all in hand? And a reminder—talk it over with your family ahead of time. Better yet, take your wife along with you to the attorney's office. Be sure you and everyone concerned knows what you want to do. In fact, it would be good public relations to let them help you improve on your own ideas of what is best.

1. Financial Advisors: Who helps you most with your personal financial affairs? What are their names and addresses? Your insurance agent, your banker, your tax accountant? Maybe you don't have much estate and maybe you seldom confer with such people. But have their names available anyway when you see your lawyer. He may want to confer with them on technical matters related to your affairs.

2. Who are your relatives? Take along a complete list of all your dependents—names, birthdates, birthplaces, relationship to you, present addresses. And if there are other relatives who may have a claim on your estate and expect something from you, especially if you have no children, or who may contribute to it some day by leaving

something to your wife or children, list them too. If you are going to mention any nonrelatives and friends in your will, be sure you have all the facts about them too.

3. Records. Make a complete list of all your important papers and where they can be found when you are gone—birth certificates, insurance policies and records, marriage certificates, car titles, real estate deeds and notes, Social Security and other pension records, savings accounts, and so forth.

4. Assets. List everything of value that you have or that you and your wife own together—money (in which banks? what kind of accounts?), savings accounts, securities, real estate, automobiles, boats, valuable collections, books, copyrights and patents, furniture, large appliances, and so on. Keep an up-to-date inventory list, adding to it as you purchase new items. List the approximate value of each item, the day you got it, how you got it, where it is, and where pertinent records related to it can be found.

5. Insurance. Make a list of all the life, health, liability, automobile, property, and other insurance policies you have. Jot down the premiums you pay, their due dates, and the benefits payable under each policy, especially death benefits. Be sure you list not only your personal policies, but those benefits to which your wife is entitled under any special church plans. If you're not sure how the proceeds of these various policies will be paid to your beneficiaries, take them along with you when you visit your lawyer.

6. Liabilities. Again, list all the debts you owe—amounts, to whom owed, due date, interest, reason for debt. If you are likely to assume any significant debts in the near future—are you planning to buy your own home?—or anticipate paying off some debts soon, make a listing of these too.

7. Distribution. While you probably intend to leave everything to your wife, you should give consideration to others in the event your wife dies before you do or at the same time. Besides, there may be some special items—heirlooms, books, specific properties, cash gifts

—which you want close friends or relatives especially to have. Make a list of who should get what.

8. Will administration. You will need someone, or perhaps even more than one person, to carry out the instructions of your will. You will need to name an executor, someone to settle your estate, list your assets and liabilities, and distribute your property as you direct. If you still have minor children, you should name a guardian. Even though a husband or wife will usually name the other, it is desirable to name someone else also in the event your wife dies with you or shortly thereafter. The executor or administrator of your estate may of course also be guardian of your minor children, as would be the case if you named your wife. In large or small estates trustees can facilitate the administration of property for beneficiaries and relieve widows of the many complexities involved. Most banks maintain excellent trust departments for this very purpose. So, before you go to work on your will, or as you are in the process of working on it, have in mind the people you would like to nominate for these responsibilities.

9. Funeral. Don't overlook the possibilities of specific directions for the disposition of your body. Be aware of the needs of others in such times. Be careful in detailing directions which may offend or hurt your survivors. Talk it over with your family. But if you are interested in donations for medical purposes, it is important to make your intentions known in your will. So discuss this with the intended recipients and your family, and then work out the details with your attorney.

10. Then, don't forget your will! An out-of-date will can be as useless as no will. Take your will out for periodic inspection to determine that events in the meantime have not changed your desires and ambitions for your beneficiaries.

A lot to do? Of course it is. But maybe these hints on estate planning—even with an estate as small as yours, be it $1,000, or $10,000, or $100,000—will suggest to you that you'd better get over to an attorney now before you waste much more time trying to write your will yourself.

Methods for Passing Property to Your Heirs

There are four ways in which you can pass property on to your heirs: (1) by a will, (2) by right of inheritance where there is no will, (3) by joint ownership, where, for instance, husband and wife own property jointly in both their names (in many states the wording of such ownership must be carefully stated), (4) by specific contract, where, for instance, a life insurance policy names a specific beneficiary. Careful use of wills and insurance will facilitate the disposition of your estate as well as minimizing fees and administrative costs.

Your will can make specific disposition of properties. Joint ownership in most states permits the survivor to receive the property for his own use without its inclusion in the deceased estate.

Insurance policies on your life may, of course, name anyone you choose as beneficiary, and the proceeds do not become part of your estate. This can be an excellent way to remember your church or your favorite institution. A $1,000 policy on your life, naming your church as irrevocable beneficiary, will cost you very little and in the meantime give your church all the benefits of cash and loan values on that policy. Besides, the premium is a deductible contribution item for your income tax return. And you have made a significant contribution to your church without jeopardizing the interests of your rightful heirs. Considerable help and guidance in matters related to items such as this can be secured from various charitable foundations and bank trust officers. Ask your attorney for specific information.

Estate and Inheritance Taxes

The amount of taxes which must be paid on the value of your estate depends on its size, on the state in which you live, on the relationship of those who have inherited from you, and on various other factors. Federal estate taxes are assessed against your estate. State inheritance taxes are usually assessed against those receiving property from your estate.

For Federal estate tax purposes, there is a $60,000 exemption for your estate. However, if you have left at least half of your estate to your wife, then the marital deduction applies and your estate must be more than $120,000 to be subject to any Federal estate tax.

Inheritance taxes are imposed by states upon the recipients of property from your estate. Tax rates and exemptions depend on amounts received as well as on the relationship of the recipient to the deceased. State laws vary on inheritance taxes, and if you are interested in the exact regulations in your state, ask your attorney.

Other Items

Other considerations which may be of interest to you as you work on your will include:

In some states holographic wills are acceptable, and no witnesses are required if you write your own will in longhand. On the other hand, you are on safer ground when you have your will typed so it is clearly legible and signed by the number of witnesses required in your state. Friends are fine for this purpose, but be sure they are likely to be easily available in the event their presence is required at the probating of your will. Two or three witnesses are usually sufficient.

Deathbed wills are acceptable in some states, but they create problems if you designate property for your church at this time or for those who have been close to you and especially helpful to you. Undue pressure and influence may be charged against these intended beneficiaries because of the near certainty of death for you and their prior associations or relationships with you. Don't wait until the last minute. Finish your will now.

Codicils are simply written provisions executed after a will has been made which add to, delete, or in any way change the provisions of the original will. While it is preferable to prepare a new will when changes are desired, if time is short, a valid codicil can be prepared in the same manner as the original will and both will be effective.

Deaths by common disasters are not as infrequent as you may think. Provisions should be made in your will for disposition of your property in the event that your wife's death should occur at the same time or soon after yours.

A Christian Writes His Will

The will of a Christian is an excellent final opportunity to complete one's stewardship of possessions as well as to make a noble confession of faith and love. As stewards of God over the possessions we have in this lifetime, we are also responsible for a proper stewardship when this life is finished for us.

You will be concerned about those you love, sympathetic to the needs of your friends and family, and you can make a tremendous witness of your faith and love through your will. Perhaps you will want to remember your church or one of its institutions or boards or agencies with a gift from your estate.

As has been said repeatedly, competent legal counsel ought to be secured whenever a will is prepared. The following example for a will, therefore, is not intended to be a final form for your will or to override any provisions which your attorney may suggest. It is presented here simply as illustrative of the various provisions which may be included in your will.

Sample of a Last Will and Testament[4]

I, _____, of the City of _____, County of _____, and State of _____, being of sound and disposing mind and memory, and under no restraint, do make and publish this my last Will and Testament, hereby revoking all wills by me heretofore made.

First, I commit myself to God's care and pray that in the hour of death my faith in him may be rich that through his love I may enjoy the heavenly mansions prepared for me through Christ's suffering and death in my behalf; and I leave those who survive me the comfort of knowing I have died in this faith.

Second, I commend those whom I love to the protecting arm of God, knowing full well that he, in my absence from them, can care for them much more adequately than I could were I present and he absent; and I encourage them to place their confidence in him richly.

ITEM I. I direct that all my just debts and funeral expenses be paid as soon as practicable after my decease.

ITEM II. I give, devise, and bequeath to _____
Church of _____, five (5) per cent of any money that may be in my possession, either to my credit in any bank or in the form of notes, bonds, mortgages, or other securities to be used by said church as its Board of Trustees may determine.

ITEM III. I give, devise, and bequeath to the _____
(denomination) Church, a corporation not for profit organized under the laws of the State of _____, and with its principal office in _____, _____, or its successors and assigns, five (5) per cent of any money that may be in my possession, either to my credit in any bank or in the form of notes, bonds, mortgages, or other securities to be used by the Corporation as its Board of Trustees may determine.

The amounts involved in Items II and III may be small, but it is my wish that they be received as an indication of my thanks to God for a life of service and happiness he has permitted me to live.

ITEM IV. I give, devise, and bequeath all of the rest and residue

---

⁴From the tract, *You Haven't Made a Will?* by the Department of Stewardship of the American Lutheran Church, 422 South Fifth Street, Minneapolis, Minnesota, and revised in 1966 under the title of *For Those You Love—Make a Will.* (While the sample would be applicable for a husband and father, the wording can easily be changed for use by a wife or, where permissible by law, for a joint last will and testament by husband and wife together.)

of my estate, both real and personal property, of every kind and description, and wheresoever situated, to my beloved wife, absolutely and in fee simple.

I make this provision in my will with full confidence that my wife will make adequate provision for our children.

ITEM V. In the event that my beloved wife, _____ should predecease me, or in the event that we are both killed or die as a result of a common disaster or accident, I give, devise, and bequeath all of the rest, residue, and remainder of my estate, both real and personal property, of every kind and description, and wheresoever situated, to our beloved children, _____,
_____, _____, and _____, absolutely and in fee simple, share and share alike.

ITEM VI. To my son, _____, I convey a father's desire that he include in his educational program a full course in a theological seminary, realizing that his developing talents and aptitudes may not point him to the ministry but knowing that such training will be helpful to him in any Christian walk of life and expecting such training to spiritually strengthen him against the evils of the day.

ITEM VII. (Appointment of executor and other items.)

IN WITNESS WHEREOF, I have hereunto subscribed my name this _____ day of _____, 19____.

_____
(Signature)

Signed and acknowledged by the said _____, as and for his Last Will and Testament, in our presence, who, at his request and in his presence, and in the presence of each other, have hereunto subscribed our names as witnesses at _____,
_____ this _____ day of _____, 19__.
_____ residing at _____
_____ residing at _____

Other Legal Documents and Papers

The complexities of today's existence require most men to keep records of a multitude of legal papers and contracts covering a wide variety of subjects, transactions, and activities. Legal documents are extremely important in today's society, and the prudent citizen will be careful to keep his "papers" in a safe and easily accessible location. Even clergymen, as citizens of the state, become just as involved in keeping these kinds of records as any one of their parishioners.

The number of documents required in a lifetime can be staggering, even for the average suburban family. But the importance of acquiring and properly maintaining these various papers cannot be overemphasized. Lost or misplaced documents can cause considerable inconvenience and possibly even the loss of rights, privileges, and property.

Safekeeping

Important documents should be kept in a safe, easily accessible, fireproof location. The logical choice is a bank safety deposit box, and the minister's family needs such safekeeping as much as anyone else. Here you can keep your will, insurance policies, real estate deeds, important contracts and agreements, cash, jewelry, and other valuables.

Safety deposit boxes are safe, fireproof, inaccessible to anyone except authorized persons you designate. The cost is small considering the security and peace of mind they give you. Different size boxes are available. Discuss your needs with your banker, and he will advise you on what to rent. But use a box before a fire or theft or other calamity destroys those valuables now stacked away in your home.

Birth Certificates

Every citizen should have documentary proof of his birth. Most of us can simply write to the courthouse of the county where we were born and secure a photostatic copy of our birth certificates. You ought to have on file for each member of your family—yourself, wife, and children—at least one copy of their birth certificates. These will be needed when the children enter school, when you apply for Social Security benefits, if you want to go out of the country, and for a variety of circumstances. Have a copy handy; it will save you considerable inconvenience and time. If you are a naturalized citizen, the same applies to copies of your naturalization papers.

If you cannot obtain a birth certificate because birth records were not kept in your home county when you were born or they have been destroyed through fire or other calamity, then you should make diligent effort to secure certified copies of your baptismal or confirmation records. Many old church records have become invaluable for documentation of birthdates and places. Eventually this information will be needed by you, and it will take time to get it. Inquire now and make sure you have proof of birth and citizenship for each member of your family whenever you are required to give it.

Automobile Records

Whenever you purchase new license plates for your car or want to sell your car or borrow money on it, you must give proof of legal ownership. You will need an accurate original or photostatic copy of your title. In some states these titles must be attached to your automobile, while in others you will want to keep them in a safe place.

You may also want to keep a file on your automobile, including records of repairs, guarantees, mileage, insurance policies, credit card account numbers, gasoline purchase receipts, and license plate receipts. If you have it all on file, then the information will be available whenever you need it.

Real Estate Papers

Purchasing and selling real property always involves legal documents. The number of such documents depends upon the complexities of the purchase or sale. But whatever is involved, you should be certain that you have all the necessary documents in your files or in your attorney's files. Deeds, contracts, mortgage notes, and all similar papers should either be in your safety deposit box or at the proper mortgage institution or with your attorney. Check with your lawyer to find out what is necessary in these matters.

Wills

Obviously your will document should be kept in a safe and easily accessible place also. Again your safety deposit box will be desirable; and while your attorney will surely have a copy in his office, the original document is necessary for probating your will. Be sure your wife or someone knows where your will is located. Since it may be necessary to examine your will even before your funeral, it ought to be available immediately upon your death.

Marriage Licenses and Related Papers

Marriage licenses and other related documents should also be kept in a safe place. Photostatic copies of all documents related to divorce, separation, child support, etc., may be secured from your courthouse and ought to be in your files. Originals, if you have them, can be kept in your safety deposit box.

Death Certificates

Photostatic copies of death certificates will almost certainly be needed for probating wills and settling estate matters. If you are involved in the administration of anyone's estate—that of your wife, or your parents, or someone else—a supply of these certificate copies will save you considerable time and expedite the completion of your responsibilities in the estate.

Insurance Policies

While all insurance companies keep a complete record of policies in force, your insurance policies are important to you and should be kept safe and accessible. Again be sure your wife or someone knows precisely where your insurance policies are kept in case of your death or incapacitation for any reason. A complete listing of all policies in force in your name would be an extremely useful schedule for your files.

Manuscripts, Sermons, and Collections

If you have ambitions for publishing your sermons or other manuscripts some day, a complete and accurate filing system ought to be developed for these. Valuable writings should be placed in a safe, fireproof file. Valuable collections of stamps or coins or other items should be properly protected and filed. Remember that one fire among your manuscripts and collections can destroy a lifetime of work. Protect them.

Tax Returns

All records related to your income tax returns should also be filed and stored in a safe place. You will do well to keep copies of your returns and related supporting information for at least five years. Of course, you will want to keep the most recent returns and supporting data easily accessible in the event you need them for referral or to support your entries if there is ever an investigation or audit of your entries.

Cancelled Checks and Bank Statements

There are differences of opinion on how long you should keep your cancelled checks and bank statements. Because you may need them to substantiate expenditures and income, they should be kept on file for several years. Find a safe place and store them for a while. You may never need them again, but if you do, you will have them available.

Bibliography

The Annuity, Today's Greatest Income Bargain, published by the Research & Review Service of America, Inc., Indianapolis, for the Metropolitan Life Insurance Co. An excellent, but brief, description of annuities—their purpose, function, and desirability.

Are You Planning on Living . . . the Rest of Your Life? U.S. Department of Health, Education, and Welfare, Administration on Aging, latest edition. An easy-to-read pamphlet describing steps one ought to take in planning for retirement—where to live, Social Security benefits, other retirement income, use of free time.

Changing Times, The Kiplinger Magazine, 1729 H Street, N.W., Washington, D.C. An excellent monthly resource magazine with a variety of articles on many topics, especially related to personal finance—family budgets, spending, investments, insurance, etc.

The Christian Family and Its Money, by David Graybeal. Board of Missions, The Methodist Church, 1963. A small book suggesting a practical approach to money management based on sound stewardship principles.

The Christian Meaning of Money, by Otto A. Piper. Prentice-Hall, Englewood, N.J., 1965. An outstanding book which evaluates the place and use of money in our kind of society. The individual and the church have a stewardship responsibility rightly to employ wealth in a manner that is charitable, humanitarian, and in accord with God's will.

A Consumer's Guide to U.S.D.A. Services. U.S. Department of Agriculture, Miscellaneous Publications No. 959, latest edition. A helpful pamphlet for families. Includes a good explanation of the many services provided consumers (not just farmers) by the U.S.D.A. including suggestions for shopping for food, controlling pests, managing family finances, caring for a home, etc. A listing of available government publications on each subject is given at the end of each chapter.

F.H.A. Homeowner's Guide. Federal Housing Administration, latest edition. A good guide to procedures required for securing F.H.A. home financing.

A Guide to Budgeting for the Young Couple. Home and Garden Bulletin No. 98, U.S. Department of Agriculture. A simplified guide for young families preparing family budgets.

Handbook for the Christian Family and Money Management. Commission on Stewardship, Lutheran Laymen's Movement for Stewardship, Lutheran Church in America, 231 Madison Ave., New York. A family money management guide to help you and your family answer the question: How can we manage our income so that its use becomes an honest expression of our highest goals? Includes forms for record keeping and budgeting.

Health Insurance for the Aged, a Brief Explanation of "Medicare." U.S. Department of Health, Education, and Welfare, Social Security Administration, latest edition. Up-to-date government information on Medicare.

How to Use Your Bank. Texas Agricultural Extension Service, College Station, Texas. An extremely simple explanation of banking services and facilities.

Investment Facts. New York Stock Exchange, latest edition. Explains in brief and simple language the function of the New York Stock Exchange, its Monthly Investment Plan, and procedures for investing in stocks. Included is a listing of common stocks on the New York Stock Exchange that have paid a cash dividend every three months for twenty to one hundred years.

Making Your Will . . . What You Should Know Before You See Your Lawyer, by Sydney Prerau. The Barton-Gillet Co., 32 S Street, Baltimore, Md. A pamphlet which describes steps that you should take before discussing with your attorney the provisions you want included in your will.

Managing Your Money, a Family Plan. Division of Home Economics, Federal Extension Service, U.S. Department of Agriculture, latest edition. A simple guide for family budgeting and spending. Includes work sheets for estimating expenses.

Minister's Federal Income Tax Guide. Published annually by the editors of *Pulpit Digest,* Channel Press, New York. An excellent manual describing in detail federal income tax and Social Security tax provisions especially applicable for ministers.

Money Management Institute Series. Household Finance Corporation, Chicago. Several booklets are available in this series including titles on budgeting, spending for home furnishings, using the food dollar, etc.

Personal Finance, by Elvin F. Donaldson and John K. Pfahl, latest edition. The Ronald Press, New York, over 700 pages. A thorough, comprehensive book explaining in detail all phases of personal finance.

Personal Finance for Clergymen, by John C. Bramer, Jr. Prentice-Hall, Inc., Englewood Cliffs, N.J., 1964. 160 pages. An overall review of personal finance planning for clergymen.

Personal Money Management, First National Bank of Minneapolis. An attractive booklet outlining a comprehensive personal money management plan including budgeting, savings, insurance and investment programming, and will or estate planning. Forms and work sheets are provided for a complete year of family record keeping.

Social Security Amendments 1965, a Brief Explanation. U.S. Department of Health, Education, and Welfare, Social Security Administration, latest edition. Up-to-date official information about recent Social Security regulations.

Social Security for Clergymen. U.S. Department of Health, Education, and Welfare, Social Security Administration, latest edition. A brief statement on Social Security regulations especially applicable for ministers.

Understanding Life Insurance for the Family. Division of Home Economics, Federal Extension Service, U.S. Department of Agriculture, latest edition. A brief, but comprehensive, description of life insurance.

What You Should Know Before You Buy a Home. The Story of Modern Home Financing. Both published by the U.S. Savings and Loan League, Chicago. Good reference materials for prospective home owners.

What Young Farm Families Should Know About Credit. Farmer's Bulletin No. 2135, U.S. Department of Agriculture, latest edition. Helpful suggestions about credit useful for city families too.

When You Use Credit . . . for the Family, Division of Home Economics, Federal Extension Service, U.S. Department of Agriculture, latest edition. An excellent description of credit—what it is, what it does, how to use it, how to compute interest costs, kinds of credit, etc.

Why You Should Choose a Family Lawyer Now! by Lester David. Prepared for the New York Life Insurance Co. and approved by the American Bar Association. A brief, helpful discussion on the importance of having a family lawyer.

List of Illustrated Forms
Useful for
Family Financial Record Keeping

INDEX